THE ST FRANCIS PRAYER BOOK

THE

PRAYER BOOK

A Guide to Deepen Your Spiritual Life

BY
JON M. SWEENEY
EDITOR OF *The Road to Assisi:*
The Essential Biography of St. Francis

PARACLETE PRESS
BREWSTER, MASSACHUSETTS

Scripture quotations from the Gospels and from "The Song of the Three Young Men" pp. 78-79 are taken from The New Jerusalem Bible, published and copyright 1985 by Darton, Longman & Todd, Ltd. and Doubleday, a division of Random House, Inc., and used by permission of the publisher.

Scripture quotations from the Psalms are taken from the *Book of Common Prayer and Administration of the Sacraments and Other Rites and Ceremonies of the Church* according to the use of the Episcopal Church copyright 1979 The Church Hymnal Corp., NY.

Scripture quotations from songs and canticles of the Hebrew scriptures and from the Apocrypha are taken from the New Revised Standard Version of the Bible copyright 1989 Division of Christian Education of the National Council of the Churches of Christ in the United States of America. Used by permission. All rights reserved.

10 9 8 7 6 5 4 3 2 1

Library of Congress Cataloging–in–Publication Data
Sweeney, Jon M., 1967-
   The St. Francis prayer book : a guide to deepen your spiritual life / by Jon M. Sweeney.
          p.   cm.
Includes bibliographical references and index.
      ISBN 1–55725–352–8 (pbk.)
 1. Catholic Church—Prayer-books and devotions—English.
2. Spiritual life—Catholic Church. 3. Francis, of Assisi,
Saint, 1182-1226. I. Title
      BX2179.F64E5 2004
      242' .802—dc22

                                                    2003024204

Published by Paraclete Press
Brewster, Massachusetts
www.paracletepress.com
Printed in the United States of America.

"My Father still goes on working, and I am at work, too."

—Our Lord Jesus Christ,
in St. John's Gospel (5:17)

CONTENTS

I
THE PRAYER LIFE OF FRANCIS OF ASSISI

II
PRAYING ALONGSIDE ST. FRANCIS

I

THE PRAYER LIFE
of
Francis of Assisi

FRANCIS AND LEO
CANNOT AGREE IN
RESPONSIVE PRAYER

*F*RANCIS was out walking one day with Brother Leo, his closest friend and companion, when it came time to pray the Divine Office. It was in the earliest days of Francis's new movement, when the brothers lived in the utmost simplicity; for this reason, and given their remote location, Francis and Leo had no books at hand when the hour for Morning Prayer had come.

Francis said to Leo: "Since we do not have a breviary with us, but it is still important that we spend time praising God, let us create something new.

"I will speak and you will answer, as I teach you.

"I will say 'O Brother Francis, you have done so many sins and evils in this world. You are deserving of hell.'

"And you, Leo, will respond, 'So it is, Francis, you deserve the lowest depths of hell.'"

Brother Leo nodded that he understood and gave Francis assurances of his perfect obedience. "Let us begin, Father," he agreed.

And so Francis began the new liturgy. He said, "You have done so many sins and evils in this world, Brother Francis, that you are deserving of hell."

"But God will work through you so much good," Leo replied earnestly, "that surely you will go to paradise."

"No, no, no," Francis said, "that is not right. When I say my part, you must say as I have instructed you, repeating, 'You are worthy only to be set among the cursed in the depths of hell.'"

Again, in obedience, Brother Leo replied, "Willingly, Father."

This time Francis paused and painfully considered his words. After a few moments, with tears in his eyes and while pounding his heart Francis said in a much louder voice: "O Lord of heaven and earth, I have done so much evil and so many sins in this world that I am worthy only to be cursed by you!"

And Leo replied in turn: "O Brother Francis, God will do great things for you and you will be blessed above all others!"

Francis was perplexed and more than a little bit angry.

"Why do you disobey me, Brother Leo? You are to repeat as I have instructed you!"

"God knows, Father," Leo answered, "that each time I set my mind to do as you say, God then makes me say what pleases him."

How could Francis argue with this? He marveled at Leo's words, searching them for the divine purpose. Nevertheless, after some time, Francis quietly said, "I pray most lovingly that you will answer me this time as I have asked you to do." Leo agreed to try, but try as he might, again and again, he could not do as Francis wished.

Time after time, into the night, past compline and throughout the early hours of the morning, the entreaties of Francis grew ever more passionate as Leo's joy grew ever larger. Their prayers never did match, and they never did agree, praying responsively as Francis had hoped.

ॐ

Francis taught the first spiritual explorers drawn to understand and imitate his life—the way to a deeper relationship with God through prayer. He showed these men and women how to pray, he gave them words to get them started, and he insisted on the dailyness of the practice. Like the first followers of the little poor man from Assisi, Francis invites us to join him in the prayer and spirituality that punctuated his life at every turn.

Francis approached God from many directions; his prayer life demonstrates the varied ways that he intertwined himself with God, through Christ, in the power of the Holy Spirit. He maintained delicate balances, such as balancing joy and song with penitence and prostration. He prayed at times in community as a leader would conduct a band in a riotous tune, but he also used prayer as form of penitence, occasionally sentencing additional prayers to those whose minds seemed idle. His prayer life was intricate and of one piece with his broad spirituality. We might also try to strike these balances in our practices of prayer. But at the very least, we should try to pray each day, perhaps many times throughout the day, with the words and spirit of Francis.

Francis viewed prayer as a tool for overcoming pride and sinfulness. For him, it was a training of the soul and body to live in eternity and not in the world. With this in mind, Francis became a champion of prayer while still a young man, and through his early experiences at prayer, he found guidance on the way to his conversion. The Spirit taught him to pray. This "inner work" never ended for Francis, as he continually saw the effects of original sin in his own life and used prayer to stamp them out.

He probably began praying in earnest in the early months of the year 1206, when he was twenty-four years old. He still lived in his father's house at this time, and it is unlikely that he received much religious instruction there. Although his mother wished a deep love of God for her only son, Francis's father, Peter Bernardone, held little respect for the Church. This was the time in Francis's life when he struggled finally to overcome his repulsion of lepers, and the filth and disease that they represented. In his final will and testament, written just before his death twenty years later, Francis connected his conversion to this time in his young adulthood.

Also at this critical stage in his life, Francis became sensitive for the first time to his need to spend time alone in quiet. A rowdy youth and king of many carnivals in Assisi, young Francis's turning away from carousing and revelry and turning toward solitude was another important stage of his receptivity to the Spirit. His prayer life could not have grown otherwise. He needed time alone to meet himself, and to meet God.

Now interested in religion, with basic capacities forming in him so that he could accept and understand its subtleties, Francis soon began to use prayer as an essential tool for discernment of the will of God in his life. When Bernard of Quintavalle, a wealthy man of Assisi, became the first to ask Francis what it might mean to follow him in his new spiritual work, the young saint insisted that they pray together at the bishop's house from early morning until terce (9 AM). Only then would they be ready to open the Scriptures together and discover the will of God.

Also early on in his religious life, Francis asked two of his most trusted friends—Brother Sylvester, the first priest to join the Order, and Sister Clare, the first woman to join the movement—to pray for him, seeking God's will for his vocation.

Francis could not discern for which purpose his life was intended. On the one hand, he felt drawn to a life of asceticism and contemplative prayer, like many religious before him, but on the other hand he felt called to a life among the people of Italy, preaching, ministering, and caring for them. Brother Sylvester and Sister Clare, after days of prayer on Francis's behalf, confirmed the latter as God's true desire, and Francis took this as if from God's very own lips. He believed in signs and in genuine intercession.

From the earliest days of his intentional spiritual life, Francis was committed to a daily prayer practice. Although he never viewed his new movement as a traditional monastic one (the early Franciscans were mendicant friars, quite distinct from cloistered monks), he nevertheless was a keeper of fixed-hour prayer, as it is often called in liturgical churches today. Cloistered monks, whose vocation is the contemplative life, sing or chant these prayers—mostly from the Psalms—in choir for hours on end each day. But because Francis never intended to stay put in one place for very long, daily prayer took on a different meaning in his movement. His prayers were peripatetic, and his spirituality was, too.

Francis maintained a regular prayer life through the praying of the Divine Office. The word "office" used in this context is from a Latin word meaning "work." This ancient form of fixed-hour prayer, also known as the Liturgy of the Hours, or the work of God, was inherited by the early Christians from Judaism. The Hebrew psalmists and the lives of the prophets (e.g., Daniel) are full of references to fixed-hour prayer—in the morning, at noon, in the evening; one psalm even says, "Seven times a day do I praise you" (Psalm 119:164). The Divine Office is distinct from the saying of the Mass, and has always been faithfully kept not just by clergy, monks, and nuns, but also by laypeople. Francis claimed this type of prayer for his vocation, and taught his followers to practice it. Regardless of his many travels—for he was forever on the road—Francis prayed "the Hours," probably remaining the most faithful to the traditional times of morning and evening prayer.

He would pray with his brothers regardless of where he was. His first biographer, Thomas of Celano, who was also a contemporary of Francis, wrote: "When he was travelling the world on foot, he always would stop walking in order to say the Hours, and when he was on horseback he would dismount to be on the ground." Many of us today find ourselves praying in the strangest of places (a stall in the restroom works well for private noontime prayers) in order to keep our everyday lives tuned to God's ear.

At this period in time, almost all prayer was spoken aloud, and at times this was difficult for Francis: "[Even when] he was suffering from diseases of the eyes, stomach, spleen, and liver, he did not want to lean against a wall or partition when he was chanting the Psalms. He always fulfilled his hours standing up straight and without a hood, without letting his eyes wander and without dropping syllables." This reminds me of the elderly couple who physically struggle but determinedly make their way to the front of our church each Sunday for the taking of Communion.

But in addition to those times when Francis would pray together with his brothers and sisters, Francis also prayed often in solitude. Contemplative prayer outside of the cloister was uncommon in Francis's day, but both Francis and many of his brothers spent hours each week alone with God. When Francis spent time alone, it was usually in order to find a more intimate, mystical communion with God. Perhaps, on these occasions, his reciting of the words of the prayer books and scriptures turned into something more, as the words of the Psalms and the Gospels became resting places for Francis in the bosom of the Unknown. Francis experienced both spoken prayers and aphasic communications with God.

His favorite places to pray alone were woods, rocky caves, cliffs, and abandoned churches. Francis, with his restless spirit, easily understood the passion of the psalmists. Sometimes a trusted friend would accompany Francis on long walks to these distant places; other times, he would set out alone. When he was quiet and alone, he sometimes prayed aloud. He would often accuse himself before God, calling himself "Vain!" and "Coward!" Francis wondered aloud to God, asking many searching questions. Who was he to have "followers"? Why hadn't God found him worthy for martyrdom when he had traveled to Syria to see the Sultan? Was his whole life a mistake? Should he have married and had children? Why had he survived serious illness when others had not? Francis came to know his own heart very well, and he accused it of every possible hint of selfishness.

Francis always returned to the most basic spiritual questions. Toward the end of his life, an eavesdropping Brother Leo overheard Francis asking plaintively: "Who are you, my dearest God? And what am I?" Unlike some more famous mystics, his contemplation never steered far from his own sinfulness.

One reason for Francis's preference to pray in seclusion was his sensitivity to avoid the appearance of showing off. He wanted to heed the warning of Jesus about hypocrites: "they love to say their prayers standing up in the synagogues [and the churches!] and at the street corners for people to see them" (Matthew 6:5). Francis also took seriously the words of Christ when he instructed his disciples to go into their room and close the door to pray. Like many of the church fathers and mothers before him, Francis probably interpreted this verse both spiritually and literally. In the spiritual sense, our prayers are times when we are alone before God; our doors are shut against worldly concerns and distractions, and we spend intimate time with our Creator, our Redeemer, our Friend. In the literal sense, a closed door brings the quiet and solitude that are necessary for proper intention and attention in prayer. Francis also surely believed, as did his contemporaries, that demons want to assail us when we pray, and demons can only know our thoughts (and hence, our prayers) if we give them verbal expression. So, we should be quiet at times and passionately inward in our prayers.

He loved to pray in the middle of the night while his brothers were asleep. At these most impassioned times, the postures of prayer became important to Francis. *The Little Flowers of St. Francis*, a collection of legends and stories from Francis's life, tells often of the saint's penitent postures in contemplative prayer. He was expressive and his movements dramatic. At times, he would beat his chest while on his knees, pounding his breast again and again as if to awaken his restive heart, and at other times he would raise his hands, lifting them as to the heavens. On one such occasion,

Francis was desperately seeking Christ through this sort of combination of spiritual, mental, and physical effort. "And at last he found Him," the text reads, "in the secret depths of his heart. And he spoke to Him reverently as to his Lord. Then he answered Him as his Judge. Next he entreated Him as a Father. Then he talked with Him as with a friend." What an extraordinary theology of prayer these lines represent.

One of the stories of Francis's nighttime prayers took place during one of his many preaching tours. He stopped on his way at a little house the brothers were using, and after joining them for the evening prayer of compline, decided to retire early with the intent of waking in the middle of the night to pray in solitude while the other brothers slept.

At this time, a young boy who had recently joined the Order was staying at the house. He had heard the wonders of their master and founder and, with childlike curiosity, he wanted to watch, listen, and understand more about St. Francis for himself.

Soon after Francis lay down to sleep on one of the mats on the floor, the young boy lay down closely beside him. The boy quietly and gently tied his tunic cord to the cord of Francis, so that when Francis arose in the middle of the night, as he was rumored to often do, the boy would feel it. When Francis woke, he saw that he was attached to the boy. Before rising, he quietly loosed the cords, leaving the lad sound asleep. Francis then left the house silently and entered the nearby woods to pray. The boy, a short time later, awoke and saw that Francis was gone. Seeing the door leading to the woods slightly ajar, he believed that his master had gone there. When he drew near and spied Francis praying in a small clearing, he saw great visions of light surrounding Francis, and saints conversing with him as with a close friend. The young boy fainted and the next he knew, Francis was carrying him in his arms, as a good shepherd does for his sheep, back to the house.

But Francis did not allow himself, or his brothers, to spend an excessive amount of time alone in contemplative prayer. He believed that there could be too much of a good thing, and that their lives were primarily intended for serving others. On one occasion, Francis confronted his friend and spiritual brother, Rufino, who had taken to contemplation so much that, over time, he had become almost mute in his love of God. He rarely spoke, and never went out to preach, as the other brothers did, for he spent all of his time in quiet meditation, absorbed in the divine mysteries. One day, Francis asked Rufino to go into Assisi and preach to the people, listening for God's inspiration. Rufino answered, "Reverend Father, please pardon me and do not send me. I do not have the gift of preaching, but am only simple and ignorant." But Francis commanded

Rufino to go, and because of his hesitance and disobedience insisted that he preach to the people in the utmost simplicity and humility—wearing only his breeches. Francis did not shy away from prescribing radical cures for spiritual ills. Rufino did as he was asked, but Francis soon joined him, also wearing only his breeches.

An idealist to be sure, Francis was never a perfectionist in prayer. He always allowed for human frailty before God and we see his own doubts and weaknesses again and again, some of them remarkably simple, like our own. On one occasion, while Francis and his three closest brothers were spending the days of Lent high atop Mount Verna in Italy, Francis had trouble waking before dawn in time for morning prayers. A combination of weariness and idleness was keeping him from his spiritual work until a mother falcon sitting on her nest near his thatched roof cell began to wake him each morning. A few minutes before matins (just before sunrise), she would make noise, waking Francis to pray. He was grateful for this outside assistance and many legends grew up around the story of that simple bird.

Francis's praying had great joy and passion, whether he was alone or with others. But prayer, even for the great St. Francis, was not always wonderful. Not only did he, like us, find it difficult at times to get out of bed in the morning in order to spend time with his Creator, but Francis's prayers were not always regular and joyful. They were occasionally full of torment. Francis spent thousands of hours throughout his life in seclusion, much of it in a thunderous silence before God. Occasionally, at these times, Francis would use fasting as a part of his prayer practice, which added bodily weariness to an already intense spiritual experience. He was also sometimes lonely, feeling isolated in his vocation. Particularly in the last few years of his life, we can observe Francis's prayer life growing most intense, as he felt that his own order was separating more and more from his original ideals.

N.ERICHSEN.

Another Story
FRANCIS AND THE YOUNG NOVICE
WHO WANTED TO OWN A
PRAYER BOOK

*O*NE DAY ST. FRANCIS was sitting before a fire when a young novice drew near to speak with him again about acquiring a psalter. The novice, knowing how passionately the master felt about Brothers Minor not owning things, was nevertheless asking again for his permission to own his own prayer book.

"Then, when you have your psalter," Francis said to him, "you will want a breviary, too. And when you own a breviary you will seat yourself in a pulpit like a great prelate and beckon to your companions, saying in a proud voice, 'Bring me my breviary!'"

Francis said this with great vivacity, like an actor in a play, motioning as a king would to his subjects. Then, taking up some cool ashes from the nearby fire, he smeared them on the forehead of the novice, saying: "There is the breviary! There is the breviary!"

Several days later, Francis was walking up and down along the roadside not far from his cell when the same young brother came to speak to him about his psalter. He asked yet again for Francis's permission to own one.

"Very well," Francis replied reluctantly and wearily. "Go on, you have only to do what your minister tells you." (This all occurred soon after Francis had lost control of his Order, and Peter of Catana was the new minister-general of the Brothers Minor.) At these words, the novice hurried away, but Francis, reflecting on what he had said, called out to the friar, crying, "Wait for me!"

Francis ran quickly to catch up with the boy, saying, "Retrace your steps a little way, I beg you. Where was I when I told you to do whatever your minister told you as to the psalter?"

They retraced their steps, as Francis had requested, finding the spot along the road near Portiuncula where their brief exchange had just taken place. Falling on his knees, there, Francis prostrated himself at the feet of the boy, crying, "Pardon, my brother, pardon, for what I said, for truly, he who would be a true Brother Minor ought to have nothing but his clothing!"

ভেউ

We see Francis's heart clearly in the story of his exchange with the young brother wanting to own a prayer book. He had an unwavering passion for Christ and knowledge from firsthand experience that it is all too easy for things to stand in the way of our full-time love of God. We, too, should examine ourselves for the obstructions that stand in our way. Most often, we have either put them there or allowed them to creep in. Even prayer books, Francis believed, such as the one you hold in your hands, can sometimes be an obstacle, rather than a ladder, to God. We can sometimes take too much comfort in the written prayers of our books, and these can become more important to us than using these same words in our lives. Francis believed that the owning of prayer books—and even the saying of prayers themselves—are not the same as relationship and intimacy with God. They are tools for our use, but by themselves they cannot produce a passion for God.

As a passionate reformer, Francis insisted that religion not be only rote, but heartfelt and true. This little prayer book is your invitation to follow Francis on his way—a unique way, to be sure, and one that is as relevant now as it was centuries ago. Francis wanted those who followed in his footsteps be the closest of friends with God, true followers of Jesus Christ, without need for anything else. Through Francis, we can learn prayer that is best made in community, but also the depths of prayer that is private and solitary. Both are necessary for a rich Christian life.

Prayer was to Francis as play is to a child—natural, easy, creative, and joyful. Before it became common to speak in personal terms of a relationship with God, Francis did so and made it seem natural. He was what we might call an intimate of the Divine. Like Moses on Mount Sinai and Jesus on Mount Tabor, he heard God's word to him with great clarity, and from an intimate distance. The Brothers Minor (which was Francis's preferred name for himself and his followers) whom he taught to pray, displayed a similar spirit. That is why Brother Giles, one of the first generation of Franciscans, was able to say with confidence: "He who does not know how to pray does not know God." The earliest followers of St. Francis knew from him that to know God is to pray; it was not supposed to be difficult.

PRAYING WITH SCRIPTURE

Many of Francis's prayers originated in the words of Scripture, because he found all of the emotions he was feeling already expressed there so clearly. Francis memorized large portions of the Bible, and he appears to have instructed his followers to do the same. He was most familiar with the Psalms and the Gospels and quoted them from memory when dictating to one of his followers a letter or an addition to the Rule, the written instruction intended to guide the spiritual and everyday life of the friars. Such memorization was common in Francis's day.*

*See the appendix to this book, "Memorization and Prayer in the Middle Ages," pp.141-143.

In Francis's time, several books were used for the praying of the Divine Office. The Psalms usually were contained in their own volume, as were the Gospels. On a few occasions, Francis insisted that he and his brothers open the book of the Gospels together in order to discern the will of God. On one such occasion, Brother Leo opened the book three times at Francis's bidding, while the master was at prayer, and each time read passages related to the Passion of Christ. Francis took this as confirmation that, as he had followed Christ in life, so he should follow Christ in some way related to his Passion. It is from this experience, in part, that we have come to understand the meaning of the stigmata in Francis's life. In fact, most of his religious life was spent giving renewed meaning— and physical expression—to the words of Jesus.

The essence of the Divine Office is the words of Scripture. We all have our favorite passages of Scripture, those that seem to "speak" directly to our hearts, and Francis had many favorites. Among his favorite psalms, for instance, was this pointed one, which he attempted to put to use when he wanted Brother Leo to pray responsively with him, in the story told at the beginning of this book:

> You have rebuked the insolent; cursed are they who stray from your commandments! *(Psalm 119:21)*

Francis loved this psalm, too, and he often repeated it to his brothers to explain why they should work with their hands:

> You shall eat the fruit of your labor;
> happiness and prosperity shall be yours.
> *(Psalm 128:2)*

He often referred to a given psalm using a kind of shorthand that was common in his day, referring to it by its first line, as when he instructed the Brothers to say the "Our Father" together with the "Out of the Depths" (Psalm 130) for the deceased:

> Out of the depths have I called to you,
>   O LORD;
> LORD, hear my voice;
>   let your ears consider well the voice of my
>   supplication
> I wait for the LORD; my soul waits for him;
>   in his word is my hope.
> My soul waits for the LORD,
>   more than watchmen for the morning,
>   more than watchmen for the morning."
> *(Psalm 130:1, 4-5)*

There was never a key moment in his life when Francis did not turn to pray. His brothers listened as he sang Psalm 142 on his death-bed:

> I cry to the LORD with my voice;
>   to the LORD I make loud supplication.

> Bring me out of prison, that I may give
>   thanks to your Name;
>   when you have dealt bountifully with me,
>   the righteous will gather around me.
>   (*Psalm 142:1, 7*)

And, of course, Francis's most popular piece of writing—"The Canticle of Brother Sun"—was composed in the style of a Hebrew psalm. Francis prayed the Psalms in the spirit of St. Augustine, one of the four great Latin Church Fathers, who said, "If the psalm prays, you pray; if it sighs, you sigh; if it rejoices, rejoice; if it hopes, hope; if it fears, fear."

Next to the Psalms, the Gospels most influenced Francis's prayer life. The teachings of Jesus spoke to the heart of Francis's vocation, informing it at every turn. Francis emulated the life of Jesus in ways that we don't easily understand today. His entire adult life, in fact, was a steady conversion of his body, soul, and spirit to the ways and words of Jesus. The Gospels were the life-blood of his prayers and spirituality.

He knew all four Gospels well, but loved Matthew's and Luke's the best, quoting from them more than twice as often as from Mark and John. He often quoted to his brothers the words of Jesus from the Gospel of Matthew, chapter 19. These were teachings of Christ for the first apostles; Francis and his brothers read them with the same sense of urgency, as they followed Christ's instructions to the letter:

> Jesus said, "If you wish to be perfect, go and sell your possessions and give the money to the poor, and you will have treasure in heaven; then come, follow me."
> *(Matthew 19:21)*

> "And everyone who has left houses, brothers, sisters, father, mother, children or land for the sake of my name will receive a hundred times as much, and also inherit eternal life."
> *(Matthew 19:29)*

Similarly, it was the words of Jesus to the first disciples that instructed the first generation of Franciscans how to grow in numbers, traveling from town to town sharing the Good News:

> "Take nothing for the journey. . . . Whatever house you enter, stay there; and when you leave let your departure be from there. . . . So they set out and went from village to village proclaiming the Good News and healing everywhere"
> *(Matthew 9:3-6).*

By following this advice, Francis's new movement spread more rapidly than anyone imagined possible.

At the same time, when too many of his countrymen were clamoring to leave everything and follow him, Francis was careful and insistent to teach that this more radical form of discipleship is not necessarily better than one where we remain as spouses, mothers, fathers, supporters of families, and members of local communities. The spirituality of St. Francis has always been available to everyone.

The following words of Jesus about servant leadership were critical to Francis's vocation. He often spoke of Matthew, chapter 20:

> Jesus called them to him and said, "You know that among the gentiles the rulers lord it over them, and great men make their authority felt. Among you this is not to happen. No; anyone who wants to become great among you must be your servant, and anyone who wants to be first among you must be your slave, just as the Son of man came not to be served but to serve, and to give him life as a ransom for many."
> (*Matthew 20:25-28*)

In addition to the Psalms and the Gospels, Francis also learned from other portions of Scripture. But not all portions of the Bible are equally represented in his written prayers and spiritual instructions. He quotes the Hebrew prophets rarely, for instance; the earliest version of his Rule contains no references to them. But in a letter that Francis composed at the end of his life to all members of the Franciscan Order, its leaders, and future leaders, he adopted a prophetic voice to make himself heard clearly. At this time, Francis had lost control of his Order, and it was headed in directions that he felt were in opposition to its original ideals. And so, in the last few years of his life, in this open letter to all of his brothers, Francis prayed like a prophet:

> If you turn to him with all your heart and with all your soul, to do what is true before him, then he will turn to you and will no longer hide his face from you.
> *(Tobit 13:6)*

> If you will not listen, if you will not lay it to heart to give glory to my name, says the LORD of hosts, then I will send the curse on you and I will curse your blessings.
> *(Malachi 2:2a)*

> Accursed is the one who is slack in doing the work of the LORD.
> *(Jeremiah 48:10)*

> Incline your ear, and come to me; listen, so that you may live.
> *(Isaiah 55:3)*

If we listen carefully, we can hear the voices of the Hebrew prophets resounding today as Francis's voice resounded in Italy in the thirteenth century.

The epistles of St. Paul and St. John also spoke directly to Francis in his new life. For example, as Jesus did before him, Francis understood keenly that a spiritual life is ultimately found in our intentions, not only in our actions. Francis taught from this passage in the first epistle of St. John:

> We know that we have passed from death to life because we love one another. Whoever does not love abides in death. All who hate a brother or sister are murderers, and you know that murderers do not have eternal life abiding in them. We know love by this, that he laid down his life for us— and we ought to lay down our lives for one another. How does God's love abide in anyone who has the world's goods and sees a brother or sister in need and yet refuses help?
> (1 John 3:14-17)

The prayer life of St. Francis was fueled by regularity, and the Scriptures were a large part of what he prayed, as well as the teachings that informed how he should pray. We, too, deepen our spiritual lives and multiply our connections to our Creator when we make daily prayer a priority in our lives. Repeated words and phrases from the Scriptures, the tested rhythms of ancient liturgical hopes and confessions, and the even more mystical communion of other believers doing the same thing around the world at the same time—which is what praying the Divine Office, or fixed-hour prayer, is all about—all serve to school us in our devotion.

II
PRAYING ALONGSIDE
St. Francis

The Daily Office
FOR SUNDAY
THROUGH SATURDAY

INTRODUCTION
MORNING AND EVENING PRAYER

THE FOLLOWING WEEKLY LITURGY is derived from various sources and reflects the concerns of Francis of Assisi. Many of the words are the same that Francis prayed and all of them are examples of the spirituality of the *Poverello*, or little poor man, from Assisi.

In his earliest Rule, Francis gave instructions to his brothers for the praying of the Divine Office. He used canticles or songs, collects, psalms, silent reflection, and the words of the Gospels themselves in his own prayer life. Similarly, in the week of daily morning and evening prayers that follow, Francis's words and ideas are our first guide.

The sequence for each day of this special morning and evening liturgy is as follows:

A. PREPARATION

B. GOSPEL SENTENCE

C. CONFESSION (as Francis instructed the Brothers for each morning and evening)

D. SILENCE (intended to be not merely pauses, but minutes of contemplation)

E. SONG OR CANTICLE (inspiring words from
   the prophets)
F. PSALM
G. GOSPEL READING
H. SILENCE
I. PRAYERS OF THE SAINTS AND THE EARLY
   FRANCISCANS
J. COLLECT (as Francis may have prayed
   with his brothers)

There are many ways that you can use these
days of morning and evening prayer in your own
prayer life. First, they are ideal as the structure for
a week-long retreat focusing on the life and
message of St. Francis. You can make such a
retreat by yourself in your own home or in a group
with others. Second, they are recommended as a
substitute for your regular prayer practice
whenever you find yourself stagnating or needing
special inspiration. For some people, this sort of
resurgence is needed one week a month, and for
others, less frequently. Third, the prayers and
readings, as they reflect the themes from Francis's
own ministry, are a good devotional supplement
to any academic or adult study of the saint.

SEVEN THEMES FOR SEVEN DAYS

SEVEN THEMES EMERGE from the life of St.
Francis, and each is the framework and subject
for one of our days of prayer.

DAY ONE *Following Christ*—the essence of Christian spirituality, and the only purpose of Francis's own life. Francis tried to follow Christ's guidelines for discipleship exactly as the original Twelve had done.

DAY TWO *Disregard for Possessions*—the first and most important rule for a true follower of Jesus, according to Francis. The first Franciscans held no personal possessions, and they also owned nothing in common. But, it is not necessary to be a friar to keep the essence of this practice. As Francis's biographer, Paul Sabatier, explains, the way of St. Francis has, from its beginnings, been open to "whoever was free at heart from all material servitude."

DAY THREE *Peace and Care in Human Relationships*—the sign of a person who has been transformed, or is becoming transformed, by the Spirit of God. As a young adult first going through the stages of conversion, Francis became sensitive in his relationships for the first time. He began to notice the outcast, give of himself to the unfortunate, deal honestly and forthrightly with the wealthy and the powerful, and use his influence to reap peace whenever and wherever he could.

DAY FOUR *Love for All Creatures*—the subject of so many legends of St. Francis. This virtue or quality is found in each of us more and more as we progress on our pilgrimage with Christ. We replace roughness toward God's creatures and Creation with a sensitivity to what is around us.

DAY FIVE *Preaching the Good News*—the primary purpose of Francis's vocation. Early in his religious life, Francis asked for intercessory prayer from Brother Sylvester and Sister Clare to ask God whether or not he should focus his life on contemplative work or active work. Sylvester and Clare confirmed that God's intention for Francis's vocation was to preach and teach. Francis's life was extraordinarily active and contemplative at the same time.

DAY SIX *Passion More Important than Learning*—a central belief of Francis. There will never be a shortage of intellectuals, but the world needs more people striving for spiritual growth and the salvation of others. Francis believed and lived that God is found more in a passionate heart than in a book.

DAY SEVEN *Joyful Simplicity*—the atmosphere of Francis's life. He surrounded his brothers, and those who he taught and cared for, with a spirit of joy for God's goodness. The essential goodness of all things, because all things are from God, is seen in simple ways, by lives lived simply. Even Francis's reaction to pain—as when he received pseudomedical treatment with fire to his face— was to find the goodness and beauty in Brother Fire, loving its goodness as he loved and revered all of God's Creation.

The Daily Office

FOR SUNDAY THROUGH SATURDAY

MORNING PRAYER
Sunday
(Theme/Intent: Following Christ)

PREPARATION

O Lord, open our lips and hear our prayer.
Light of the world,
shine through our lives this day.
Our mouths shall proclaim your glory.
Praise the Lord! Alleluia!

GOSPEL SENTENCE

Matthew 22:37-40

OUR LORD JESUS CHRIST, SAYS; You must love the Lord your God with all your heart, with all your soul, and with all your mind. This is the greatest and the first commandment. The second resembles it: You must love your neighbor as yourself. On these two commandments hang the whole Law, and the Prophets too.

Have Mercy on Me, O God
(from Psalm 51)

Have mercy on me, O God,
   according to your loving-kindness;
   in your great compassion blot out my offenses.
Wash me through and through from my
   wickedness and cleanse me from my sin.
For I know my transgressions,
   and my sin is ever before me.
Create in me a clean heart, O God,
   and renew a right spirit within me.
Cast me not away from your presence
   and take not your holy Spirit from me.
Give me the joy of your saving help again
   and sustain me with your bountiful Spirit.
Deliver me from death, O God,
   and my tongue shall sing of your righteousness,
   O God of my salvation.

SILENCE

The Song of Hannah

1 Samuel 2:1, 5, 7-8

REFRAIN
My heart exults in the LORD;
my strength is exalted in my God.
The pillars of the earth are the LORD'S,
and on them he has set the world.

My heart exults in the LORD;
my strength is exalted in my God.
Those who were full have hired themselves out
for bread,
but those who were hungry are fat with spoil.
The barren has borne seven, but she who has
many children is forlorn.
The LORD makes poor and makes rich;
he brings low, he also exalts.
He raises up the poor from the dust;
and lifts the needy from the ash heap,
to make them sit with princes and inherit a
seat of honor.
For the pillars of the earth are the LORD'S,
and on them he has set the world.

My heart exults in the LORD;
my strength is exalted in my God.
The pillars of the earth are the LORD'S,
and on them he has set the world.

Psalm 108:1-5

My heart is firmly fixed, O God, my heart is fixed;
  I will sing and make melody.
Wake up, my spirit; awake, lute and harp;
  I myself will waken the dawn.
I will confess you among the peoples, O lord;
  I will sing praises to you among the nations.
For your loving-kindness is greater than the heavens,
  and your faithfulness reaches to the clouds.
Exalt yourself above the heavens, O God,
  and your glory over all the earth.

GOSPEL READING

Matthew 22:1-5a, 8-14

HEAR THE WORD OF THE LORD: Jesus began to speak to them in parables once again, 'The kingdom of Heaven may be compared to a king who gave a feast for his son's wedding. He sent his servants to call those who had been invited, but they would not come. Next he sent some more servants with the words, "Tell those who have been invited: Look, my banquet is all prepared, my oxen and fattened cattle have been slaughtered, everything is ready. Come to the wedding.' But they were not interested. . . . Then he said to his servants, 'The wedding is ready; but as those who were invited proved to be unworthy, go to the main crossroads and invite everyone you can find to come to the wedding.' So these servants went out into the roads and collected together everyone they could find, bad and good alike; and the wedding hall was filled with guests. When the king came in to look at the guests he noticed one man who was not wearing a wedding garment, and said to him, 'How did you get in here, my friend, without a wedding garment?' And the man was silent. Then the king said to the attendants, 'Bind his hand and foot and throw him into the darkness outside, where there will be weeping and grinding of teeth.' For many are invited but not all are chosen."

SILENCE

PRAYERS OF THE SAINTS

Pierce, O most sweet Lord Jesus, my inmost soul with the most joyous and healthful wound of your love, and with true, calm, and most holy apostolic charity, that my soul may ever languish and melt with entire love and longing for you, may yearn for you and for your courts, may long to be dissolved and to be with you. Grant that my soul may hunger after you, the Bread of Angels, the refreshment of holy souls, our daily and supersubstantial bread, having all sweetness and savor and every delightful taste.

—*St. Bonaventure,*
minister general of the Brothers Minor

COLLECT

Blessed Holy Physician,
who heals the sick and removes the offending limb,
at home both in heaven and on earth.
Save us, O Holy One,
we who are sick and ailing;
Our wounds are deep, our hearts heavy,
and your medicine heavenly. Amen.

EVENING PRAYER
Sunday
(Theme/Intent: Following Christ)

PREPARATION

O Lamb of God,
that takes away the sins of the world,
have mercy upon us.
O Lamb of God,
that takes away the sins of the world,
grant us thy peace.

GOSPEL SENTENCE

Matthew 16:24-26

OUR LORD JESUS CHRIST, SAYS: If anyone wants
to be a follower of mine, let him renounce himself
and take up his cross and follow me. Anyone who
wants to save his life will lose it; but anyone who
loses his life for my sake will find it. What, then,
will anyone gain by winning the whole world and
forfeiting his life?

CONFESSION

The *Our Father*
(Matthew 6:9-13)

Our Father in heaven,
may your name be held holy,
your kingdom come, your will be done,
on earth as in heaven.
Give us today our daily bread.
And forgive us our debts,
as we have forgiven those who are in debt to us.
And do not put us to the test,
but save us from the Evil One.

SILENCE

SONG OR CANTICLE
(sung, when possible; otherwise, spoken aloud with feeling)

Judith's Song of Praise
Judith 16:13-16

REFRAIN
For every sacrifice as a fragrant offering is a small thing.
But whoever fears the lord is great for ever.

I will sing to my God a new song.
O LORD, you are great and glorious, wonder in
strength, invincible.

Let all your creatures serve you, for you spoke,
and they were made.
You sent forth your spirit, and it formed them;
there is none that can resist your voice.
For the mountains shall be shaken to their
foundations with the waters; before your
glance the rocks shall melt like wax.
But to those who fear you you show mercy.
For every sacrifice as a fragrant offering is a small
thing, and the fat of all whole burnt offerings
to you is a very little thing;
but whoever fears the LORD is great forever.

For every sacrifice as a fragrant offering is a small thing.
But whoever fears the lord is great for ever.

Psalm 22:2-11

O my God, I cry in the daytime,
but you do not answer;
by night as well, but I find no rest.
Yet you are the Holy One,
enthroned upon the praises of Israel.
Our forefathers put their trust in you;
they trusted, and you delivered them.
They cried out to you and were delivered;
they trusted in you and were not put to shame.

But as for me, I am a worm and no man,
  scorned by all and despised by the people.
All who see me laugh me to scorn;
  they curl their lips and wag their heads, saying,
"He trusted in the LORD; let him deliver him;
  let him rescue him, if he delights in him."
Yet you are he who took me out of the womb,
  and kept me safe upon my mother's breast.
I have been entrusted to you ever since I was born;
  you were my God when I was still in my
  mother's womb.
Be not far from me, for trouble is near,
  and there is none to help.

GOSPEL READING

Matthew 13:44-46

HEAR THE WORD OF THE LORD: The kingdom of
Heaven is like treasure hidden in a field which
someone has found; he hides it again, goes off in
his joy, sells everything he owns and buys the
field. Again, the kingdom of Heaven is like a
merchant looking for fine pearls; when he finds
one of great value he goes and sells everything he
owns and buys it.

SILENCE

PRAYERS OF THE SAINTS

Christ, be with me, Christ within me,
   Christ behind me, Christ before me,
Christ beside me, Christ to win me,
   Christ to comfort and restore me,
Christ beneath me, Christ above me,
   Christ in quiet, Christ in danger,
Christ in hearts of all that love me,
   Christ in mouth of friend and stranger.
   Amen.
   —*St. Patrick, apostle of Ireland*

COLLECT

Glorious God our Father,
like old Simeon in the temple, our eyes
have seen your salvation.
You have prepared it in the presence
of all people, a light—as we ourselves should be—
a revelation to the Gentiles and
glory to your people Israel. Amen.

MORNING PRAYER
Monday

(Theme/Intent: Disregard for Possessions)

PREPARATION

In the morning we call out to you, O Lord.
We offer our hands, our feet, our minds,
our hearts, and our souls to you this day.

GOSPEL SENTENCE

Matthew 6:19-21

OUR LORD JESUS CHRIST, SAYS: Do not store up
treasures for yourselves on earth, where moth and
woodworm destroy them and thieves can break in
and steal. But store up treasures for yourselves in
heaven. . . . For wherever your treasure is, there
will your heart be too.

CONFESSION

Have Mercy on Me, O God
(from Psalm 51)

Have mercy on me, O God,
   according to your loving-kindness;
   in your great compassion blot out my offenses.
Wash me through and through from my
  wickedness and cleanse me from my sin.
For I know my transgressions,
  and my sin is ever before me.
Create in me a clean heart, O God,
  and renew a right spirit within me.
Cast me not away from your presence
  and take not your holy Spirit from me.
Give me the joy of your saving help again
  and sustain me with your bountiful Spirit.
Deliver me from death, O God,
  and my tongue shall sing of your righteousness,
  O God of my salvation.

SILENCE

Isaiah's Second Song
(Isaiah 55:1-3, 6)

REFRAIN
Why do you spend your money
for that which is not bread,
and your labor for that which does not satisfy?

Ho, everyone who thirsts, come to the waters;
and you that have no money,
come, buy and eat!
Come, buy wine and milk without money and
without price.
Why do you spend your money for that which
is not bread,
and your labor for that which does not satisfy?
Listen carefully to me, and eat what is good,
and delight yourselves in rich food.
Incline your ear, and come to me; listen, so
that you may live.
Seek the LORD while he may be found, call
upon him while he is near.

Why do you spend your money
for that which is not bread,
and your labor for that which does not satisfy?

Psalm 95:1-7

Come, let us sing to the LORD;

    let us shout for joy to the Rock of our salvation.

Let us come before his presence with thanksgiving

    and raise a loud shout to him with psalms.

For the LORD is a great God,

    and a great King above all gods.

In his hand are the caverns of the earth,

    and the heights of the hills are his also.

The sea is his, for he made it,

    and his hands have molded the dry land.

Come, let us bow down, and bend the knee,

    and kneel before the LORD our Maker.

For he is our God,

    and we are the people of his pasture and the
    sheep of his hand.

Oh, that today you would hearken to his voice!

GOSPEL READING

Luke 12:15-21

HEAR THE WORD OF THE LORD: Jesus said to them, "Watch, and be on your guard against avarice of any kind, for life does not consist in possessions, even when someone has more than he needs." Then he told them a parable, "There was once a rich man who, having had a good harvest from his land, thought to himself, 'What am I to do? I have not enough room to store my crops.' Then he said, 'This is what I will do: I will pull down my barns and build bigger ones, and store all my grain and my goods in them, and I will say to my soul: My soul, you have plenty of good things laid by for many years to come; take things easy, eat, drink, have a good time.' But God said to him, 'Fool! This very night the demand will be made for your soul; and this hoard of yours, whose will it be then?' So it is when someone stores up treasure for himself instead of becoming rich in the sight of God."

SILENCE

O Lord, save your people, and bless your inheritance. Govern them and lift them up forever. Day by day we magnify you; we worship your name forever. Keep us this day from all sin. O Lord, have mercy on us. O Lord, show us mercy as we put our trust in you. O Lord, our hope is in you; our hope is not in vain.

—*Nicetas, fifth-century bishop of Remesiana*

COLLECT

Most High, glorious God,
enlighten the shadows of our hearts.
Grant us a right faith,
a certain hope,
and perfect charity, sense, and understanding,
so that we may accomplish
your holy and true command. Amen.

EVENING PRAYER
Monday
(Theme/Intent: Disregard for Possessions)

PREPARATION

In the evening we call out to you, O Lord.
We offer our prayers, ourselves, to you this night.
May our words and our intentions rise up.
Incline your ear to hear us.

GOSPEL SENTENCE

Matthew 19:21

OUR LORD JESUS CHRIST, SAYS: If you wish to be
perfect, go and sell your possessions and give the
money to the poor, and you will have treasure in
heaven; then come, follow me.

The *Our Father*
(Matthew 6:9-13)

Our Father in heaven,
may your name be held holy,
your kingdom come, your will be done,
on earth as in heaven.
Give us today our daily bread.
And forgive us our debts,
as we have forgiven those who are in debt to us.
And do not put us to the test,
but save us from the Evil One.

SILENCE

SONG OR CANTICLE
(sung, when possible, or spoken aloud with feeling)

Isaiah's Song for Deliverance
(Isaiah 12:2-5)

REFRAIN
Sing praises to the LORD,
for he has done gloriously;
let this be known in all the earth.

Surely God is my salvation;
I will trust, and will not be afraid,

for the LORD GOD is my strength and my might;
    he has become my salvation.
With joy you will draw water from the wells
    of salvation. And you will say on that day:
Give thanks to the LORD, call on his name;
    make known his deeds among the nations;
    proclaim that his name is exalted.
Sing praises to the LORD,
    for he has done gloriously;
    let this be known in all the earth.

> Sing praises to the LORD,
> for he has done gloriously;
> let this be known in all the earth.

PSALM
(chanted, when possible; otherwise, spoken aloud)

Psalm 100

Be joyful in the LORD, all you lands;
    serve the LORD with gladness
    and come before his presence with a song.
Know this: The LORD himself is God;
    he himself has made us and we are his;
    we are his people and the sheep of his pasture.
Enter his gates with thanksgiving;
    go into his courts with praise;
    give thanks to him and call upon his Name.

For the LORD is good;
   his mercy is everlasting;
   and his faithfulness endures from age to age.

GOSPEL READING

Matthew 19:23-26

HEAR THE WORD OF THE LORD: Then Jesus said to his disciples, "In truth I tell you, it is hard for someone rich to enter the kingdom of Heaven. Yes, I tell you again, it is easier for a camel to pass through the eye of a needle than for someone rich to enter the kingdom of Heaven." When the disciples heard this they were astonished. "Who can be saved, then?" they said. Jesus gazed at them. "By human resources," he told them, "this is impossible; for God everything is possible."

SILENCE

PRAYERS OF THE SAINTS

Lord, you are not seen except by the pure of heart. I seek by reading and meditating what is true purity of heart and how it may be had, so

that with its help I may know you, if only a little.
Lord, for long have I meditated in my heart, seeking
to see your face. It is the sight of you, Lord, that
I have sought; and all the while in my meditation
the fire of longing, the desire to know you more
fully, has increased. . . . So give me, Lord, some
pledge of what I hope to inherit, at least one drop
of heavenly rain with which to refresh my thirst,
for I am on fire with love. Amen.

    —*Guigo the Carthusian*

COLLECT

Blessed Lady Poverty,
hidden from the eyes of the world,
a pearl priceless and beautiful.
Guide us, our Lady,
we your simple ones,
for the road is difficult
and the gate at the end is narrow. Amen.

MORNING PRAYER
Tuesday
(Theme/Intent:
Peace and Care in Human Relationships)

PREPARATION

Blessed Jesus,
heaven and earth praise you.
You are worthy of every praise and honor.
Children of God, praise the Lord.
We are all God's children.
Praise! Praise!

GOSPEL SENTENCE

John 13:34-35

OUR LORD JESUS CHRIST, says: I give you a new commandment: love one another; you must love one another just as I have loved you. It is by your love for one another, that everyone will recognize you as my disciples.

Have Mercy on Me, O God
(from Psalm 51)

Have mercy on me, O God, according to your
  loving-kindness;
  in your great compassion blot out my offenses.
Wash me through and through from me wickedness
  and cleanse me from my sin.
For I know my transgressions,
  and my sin is ever before me.
Create in me a clean heart, O God,
  and renew a right spirit within me.
Cast me not away from your presence
  and take not your holy Spirit from me.
Give me the joy of your saving help again
  and sustain me with your bountiful Spirit.
Deliver me from death, O God,
  and my tongue shall sing of your righteousness,
  O God of my salvation.

SILENCE

Tobit's Hymn for Repentance
Tobit 13:1-6a

REFRAIN
Exalt God in the presence of every living being,
  because he is our LORD and he is our God.

Blessed be God who lives forever, because his
  kingdom lasts throughout all ages.
For he afflicts, and he shows mercy; he leads
  down to Hades in the lowest regions of the earth,
and he brings up from the great abyss, and
  there is nothing that can escape his hand.
Acknowledge him before the nations,
  O children of Israel;
for he has scattered you among them. He has
  shown you his greatness even there.
Exalt him in the presence of every living being,
because he is our LORD and he is our God;
  he is our Father and he is God forever.
He will afflict you for your iniquities, but he
  will again show mercy on all of you.
He will gather you from all the nations among
  whom you have been scattered.
If you turn to him with all your heart and
  with all your soul, to do what is true before him,
then he will turn to you and will no longer
  hide his face from you.

  Exalt God in the presence of every living being,
  because he is our LORD and he is our God.

Psalm 42:1-7

As the deer longs for the water-brooks,
  so longs my soul for you, O God.
My soul is athirst for God,
  athirst for the living God;
  when shall I come to appear before the
  presence of God?
My tears have been my food day and night,
  while all day long they say to me,
  "Where now is your God?"
I pour out my soul when I think on these things:
  how I went with the multitude and led them
  into the house of God,
With the voice of praise and thanksgiving,
  among those who keep holy-day.
Why are you so full of heaviness, O my soul?
  and why are you so disquieted within me?
Put your trust in God;
  for I will yet give thanks to him, who is the
  help of my countenance, and my God.

John 13:3-5, 12-15

HEAR THE WORD OF THE LORD: Jesus knew that the Father had put everything into his hands, and that he had come from God and was returning to God, and he got up from table, removed his outer garments and, taking a towel, wrapped it round his waist; he then poured water into a basin and began to wash the disciples' feet and to wipe them with the towel he was wearing. . . . When he had washed their feet and put on his outer garments again he went back to the table. "Do you understand," he said, "what I have done to you? You call me Master and Lord, and rightly; so I am. If I, then, the Lord and Master, have washed your feet, you must wash each other's feet. I have given you an example so that you may copy what I have done to you."

SILENCE

Christian, learn from Christ how you ought to love Christ. Learn a love that is tender, wise, strong; love with tenderness, not passion, wisdom, not foolishness, and strength, lest you become weary and turn away from the love of the Lord. . . . Let your love be strong and constant, neither yielding to fear nor cowering at hard work. Let us love affectionately, discreetly, intensely. We know that the love of the heart, which is affectionate, is sweet indeed, but liable to be led astray if it lacks the love of the soul. Amen.

—*St. Bernard of Clairvaux*

COLLECT

Abba, Father,
cleanse our hearts of sin this day,
reminding us that love is more
powerful than knowledge or judgment.
Fill our weak vessels with the
fruits of righteousness,
through Jesus Christ,
for your glory and honor. Amen.

EVENING PRAYER

Tuesday

(Theme/Intent:
Peace and Care in Human Relationships)

PREPARATION

O Christ, have mercy upon us.
O Christ, save us from our sins.
Our mouths shall proclaim your praise.
Praise the Lord! Alleluia!

GOSPEL SENTENCE

Matthew 7:12

OUR LORD JESUS CHRIST, SAYS: So always treat others as you would like them to treat you; that is the Law and the Prophets.

The *Our Father*
(Matthew 6:9-13)

Our Father in heaven,
may your name be held holy,
your kingdom come, your will be done,
on earth as in heaven.
Give us today our daily bread.
And forgive us our debts,
as we have forgiven those who are in debt to us.
And do not put us to the test,
but save us from the Evil One.

SILENCE

SONG OR CANTICLE
(sung, when possible; otherwise, spoken aloud with feeling)

Tobit's Hymn of Blessing
Tobit 13:14-16a

REFRAIN
My soul blesses the LORD, the great King!

Happy are those who love you, and happy are
those who rejoice in your prosperity.

Happy also are all people who grieve with you
    because of your afflictions;
for they will rejoice with you and witness all
    your glory forever.
My soul blesses the LORD, the great King!
For Jerusalem will be built as his house for all ages.
How happy I will be if a remnant of my
    descendants should survive
to see your glory and acknowledge the King of
    heaven.

My soul blesses the LORD, the great King!

PSALM
(chanted, when possible; otherwise, spoken aloud)

Psalm 146

Hallelujah!
Praise the LORD, O my soul!
    I will praise the LORD as long as I live;
    I will sing praises to my God while I have
    my being.
Put not your trust in rulers, nor in any child
    of earth,
    for there is no help in them.
When they breathe their last,
    they return to earth,
    and in that day their thoughts perish.

Happy are they who have the God of Jacob
for their help!
whose help is in the LORD their God;
Who made heaven and earth, the seas,
and all that is in them;
who keeps his promise for ever;
Who gives justice to those who are oppressed,
and food to those who hunger.
The LORD sets the prisoners free;
the LORD opens the eyes of the blind;
the LORD lifts up those who are bowed down;
The LORD loves the righteous;
the LORD cares for the stranger;
he sustains the orphan and widow,
but frustrates the way of the wicked.
The LORD shall reign for ever,
your God, O Zion, throughout all generations.
Hallelujah!

GOSPEL READING

Matthew 20:25-28

HEAR THE WORD OF THE LORD: Jesus called the
disciples to him and said, "You know that among
the gentiles the rulers lord it over them, and great
men make their authority felt. Among you this is
not to happen. No; anyone who wants to become
great among you must be your servant, and anyone

who wants to be first among you must be your slave, just as the Son of man came not to be served but to serve, and to give his life as a ransom for many."

SILENCE

PRAYERS OF THE SAINTS

Holy and blessed One,
help the spring of radiant love that fills our
   hearts to gush forth.
Jesus in our hearts,
Jesus in our mouths,
   Jesus in our ears,
Jesus in our eyes,
Jesus in our hands,
as we make our way in the world. Amen.
     —*Brother Thomas of Celano*
     (adapted from his *Life of Saint Francis*, II, ix)

COLLECT

Almighty and merciful God,
You know the desires of our hearts;
our greatest desire is to love you more completely.
We also yearn to know our neighbor,
to be your presence to both friends and strangers.
Show us your light and your wisdom,
through Jesus Christ our Lord.
Amen.

MORNING PRAYER
Wednesday

(Theme/Intent: Love for All Creatures)

PREPARATION

O Lord, our shepherd:
You revive our soul, you guide our path,
and save us from death each day.
We always want to be in your company.

GOSPEL SENTENCE

John 6:63

OUR LORD JESUS CHRIST, SAYS: It is the spirit that gives life, the flesh has nothing to offer. The words I have spoken to you are spirit and they are life.

CONFESSION

Have Mercy on Me, O God
(from Psalm 51)

Have mercy on me, O God,
  according to your loving-kindness;
  in your great compassion blot out my offenses.
Wash me through and through from my
  wickedness and cleanse me from my sin.
For I know my transgressions,
  and my sin is ever before me.
Create in me a clean heart, O God,
  and renew a right spirit within me.
Cast me not away from your presence
  and take not your holy Spirit from me.
Give me the joy of your saving help again
  and sustain me with your bountiful Spirit.
Deliver me from death, O God,
  and my tongue shall sing of your righteousness,
  O God of my salvation.

SILENCE

Sing a New Song
Isaiah 42:10-12; 43:1-3a

REFRAIN
Sing to the LORD a new song,
his praise from the end of the earth!

Sing to the LORD a new song, his praise from
the end of the earth!
Let the sea roar and all that fills it, the coastlands
and their inhabitants.
Let the desert and its towns lift up their voice,
the villages that Kedar inhabits;
let the inhabitants of Sela sing for joy, let them
shout from the tops of the mountains.
Let them give glory to the LORD, and declare
his praise in the coastlands.
But now thus says the LORD, he who created you,
O Jacob, he who formed you, O Israel:
Do not fear, for I have redeemed you;
I have called you by name, you are mine.
When you pass through the waters,
I will be with you; and through the rivers,
they shall not overwhelm you;
when you walk through fire you shall not be
burned, and the flame shall not consume you.
For I am the LORD your God,
the Holy One of Israel, your Savior.

Sing to the LORD a new song,
his praise from the end of the earth!

Psalm 84:1-7

How dear to me is your dwelling,
   O LORD of hosts!
My soul has a desire and longing for the
   courts of the LORD;
   my heart and my flesh rejoice in the living God.
The sparrow has found her a house
   and the swallow a nest where she may lay her
   young;
   by the side of your altars, O LORD of hosts,
   my King and my God.
Happy are they who dwell in your house!
   they will always be praising you.
Happy are the people whose strength is in you!
   whose hearts are set on the pilgrims' way.
Those who go through the desolate valley
   will find it a place of springs,
   for the early rains have covered it with pools
   of water.
They will climb from height to height,
   and the God of gods will reveal himself
   in Zion.
LORD God of hosts, hear my prayer;
   hearken, O God of Jacob.

Matthew 5:1-10

HEAR THE WORD OF THE LORD: Seeing the crowds, he went onto the mountain. And when he was seated his disciples came to him. Then he began to speak. This is what he taught them:

How blessed are the poor in spirit:
  the kingdom of Heaven is theirs.
Blessed are the gentle:
  they shall have the earth as inheritance.
Blessed are those who mourn:
  they shall be comforted.
Blessed are those who hunger and thirst for
  uprightness: they shall have their fill.
Blessed are the merciful:
  they shall have mercy shown them.
Blessed are the pure in heart: they shall see God.
Blessed are the peacemakers:
  they shall be recognised as children of God.
Blessed are those who are persecuted in the cause
  of uprightness: the kingdom of Heaven is theirs.

SILENCE

The most wondrous thought of all is: In this dreadful deed of the Passion committed against the Innocent One, he furnished an example of patience; he taught the truth to those who slew him, and with cries and tears did pray to the Father for them, and in return for this greatest of sins (for which the whole world and human nature deserved to perish), he bestowed on them the greatest benefits. By the pain and suffering they inflicted on him he saved them from pain and suffering. He opened the gates of Paradise to those who crucified him and to all others, reconciling them to the Father, and such grace did he obtain for us that we are to become the Sons of God. Amen.

—*Blessed Angela of Foligno*

COLLECT

Bless the Lord
living and true!
Let us give God praise,
glory, honor, and all good!
Amen.
Amen!
So be it.
So be it!

EVENING PRAYER
Wednesday

(Theme/Intent: Love for All Creatures)

PREPARATION

Almighty and everlasting God, at evening, and morning, and noonday, we humbly ask your majesty that you would drive from our hearts the darkness of sins and make us to come to the true Light, which is Christ, through Jesus Christ our Lord.

GOSPEL SENTENCE

John 6:51

OUR LORD JESUS CHRIST, SAYS: I am the living bread which has come down from heaven. Anyone who eats this bread will live for ever; and the bread that I shall give is my flesh, for the life of the world.

CONFESSION

Trisagion, an ancient Lenten prayer
(said three times)

Holy God,
Holy and Mighty,
Holy Immortal One,
Have mercy upon us.

SILENCE

SONG OR CANTICLE
(sung, when possible, or spoken aloud with feeling)

Song of the Three Young Men
Daniel 3:57, 74-82

REFRAIN
Bless the Lord, all the Lord's creation:
praise and glorify him for ever!

Let the earth bless the Lord: praise and glorify
him for ever!
Bless the Lord, mountains and hills,
praise and glorify him for ever!
Bless the Lord, springs of water, seas and
rivers, whales and everything that moves in
the waters, praise and glorify him for ever!

Bless the Lord every kind of bird, praise and
   glorify him for ever!
Bless the Lord, all animals wild and tame,
   praise and glorify him for ever!
Bless the Lord, all the human race:
   praise and glorify him for ever!

> Bless the Lord, all the Lord's creation:
> praise and glorify him for ever!

PSALM

(chanted, when possible; otherwise, spoken aloud)

Psalm 141:1-3, 8

O LORD, I call to you; come to me quickly;
   hear my voice when I cry to you.
Let my prayer be set forth in your sight as incense,
   the lifting up of my hands as the evening
   sacrifice.
Set a watch before my mouth, O LORD,
   and guard the door of my lips;
   let not my heart incline to any evil thing.
My eyes are turned to you, LORD God;
   in you I take refuge;
   do not strip me of my life.

Matthew 5:13-16

HEAR THE WORD OF THE LORD: JESUS SAID, "You are salt for the earth. But if salt loses its taste, what can make it salty again? It is good for nothing, and can only be thrown out to be trampled under people's feet. You are light for the world. A city built on a hill-top cannot be hidden. No one lights a lamp to put it under a tub; they put it on the lamp-stand where it shines for everyone in the house. In the same way your light must shine in people's sight, so that, seeing your good works, they may give praise to your Father in heaven."

SILENCE

Sweet, incomparable love, you are Christ. You are love that joins friends who fight; love that anoints wounds and cures them; love that pardons those who offend you and crown with glory those who know how to humble themselves.

Sweet and delicate love, you are the uncreated Divine. You make the seraphim flame with your glory; you make cherubim, apostles, and martyrs happy; you draw prophets from the devil's net.

We have such thirst for you, sweet love, and may it never be satisfied. Amen.

—*Brother Jacopone of Todi*

COLLECT

O holy One,
whose Son is our Good Shepherd,
watching for us when we stray,
keeping us close at hand, we pray:
Show us the way of gentleness,
love, and care for all of your creatures,
that we may see your Spirit, and heed
its holy presence, in all things created
by your hand. Amen.

MORNING PRAYER
Thursday

(Theme/Intent: Preaching the Good News)

PREPARATION

Make us, O Lord, to flourish like pure lilies
in the courts of your house,
and to show to the faithful the fragrance of good
works and the example of a godly life,
through your mercy.

GOSPEL SENTENCE

Matthew 11:28-29

OUR LORD JESUS CHRIST, SAYS: Come to me, all
you who labour and are overburdened, and I will
give you rest. Shoulder my yoke and learn from
me, for I am gentle and humble in heart, and you
will find rest for your souls.

Have Mercy on Me, O God
(from Psalm 51)

Have mercy on me, O God,
   according to your loving-kindness;
   in your great compassion blot out my offenses.
Wash me through and through from my
   wickedness and cleanse me from my sin.
For I know my transgressions,
   and my sin is ever before me.
Create in me a clean heart, O God,
   and renew a right spirit within me.
Cast me not away from your presence
   and take not your holy Spirit from me.
Give me the joy of your saving help again
   and sustain me with your bountiful Spirit.
Deliver me from death, O God,
   and my tongue shall sing of your righteousness,
   O God of my salvation.

SILENCE

God's Calling
Ezekiel 36:24-28

REFRAIN
A new heart I will give you,
and a new spirit I will put within you.

I will take you from the nations, and gather
    you from all the countries,
    and bring you into your own land.
I will sprinkle clean water upon you, and you
    shall be clean from all
your uncleannesses, and from all your idols
    I will cleanse you.
A new heart I will give you, and a new spirit
    I will put within you;
and I will remove from your body the heart of
    stone and give you a heart of flesh.
I will put my spirit within you,
    and make you follow my statutes
    and be careful to observe my ordinances.
Then you shall live in the land that I gave to
    your ancestors;
and you shall be my people,
    and I will be your God.

A new heart I will give you,
and a new spirit I will put within you.

Psalm 24:1-6

The earth is the LORD's and all that is in it,
the world and all who dwell therein.
For it is he who founded it upon the seas
and made it firm upon the rivers of the deep.
"Who can ascend the hill of the LORD?
and who can stand in his holy place?"
"Those who have clean hands and a pure heart,
who have not pledged themselves to falsehood,
nor sworn by what is a fraud.
They shall receive a blessing from the LORD
and a just reward from the God of their salvation."
Such is the generation of those who seek him,
of those who seek your face, O God of Jacob.

GOSPEL READING

Luke 9:57-62

HEAR THE WORD OF THE LORD: As they travelled along they met a man on the road who said to him, "I will follow you wherever you go." Jesus answered, "Foxes have holes and the birds of the air have nests, but the Son of man has nowhere to lay his head." Another to whom he said, "Follow me," replied, "Let me go and bury my father first." But he answered, "Leave the dead to bury their dead; your duty is to go and spread the news of the kingdom of God." Another said, "I will follow you, sir, but first let me go and say good-bye to my people at home." Jesus said to him, "Once the hand is laid on the plough, no one who looks back is fit for the kingdom of God."

SILENCE

PRAYERS OF THE SAINTS

In the mighty power of God, who is both God and human, and in every place—for his power extends everywhere—the faithful must be empowered by the four Evangelists, pondering God's precepts and filled with virtuous prudence, so that they may understand from where they've come and what they will become. For God is fire, and his angels, from time to time, announce to humankind his miracles and the wonders of his throne. They are burning spirits, who shine before his face and who are so on fire in their love for him that they desire nothing other than what he wishes. Amen.

　—*St. Hildegard of Bingen*

COLLECT

(the Agnus Dei)

O Lamb of God,
    that takes away the sins of the world,
    have mercy upon us.
O Lamb of God,
    that takes away the sins of the world,
    have mercy upon us.
O Lamb of God,
    that takes away the sins of the world,
    grant us thy peace.

EVENING PRAYER
Thursday

(Theme/Intent: Preaching the Good News)

PREPARATION

Blessed Lord,
anoint our lips;
seal them with your holy touch;
breathe fire into our quiet hearts,
that we may praise you,
and sing your praises to the world.

GOSPEL SENTENCE

Matthew 10:16

OUR LORD JESUS CHRIST, SAYS: Look, I am sending
you out like sheep among wolves; so be cunning
as snakes and yet innocent as doves.

CONFESSION

The *Our Father*
(Matthew 6:9-13)

Our Father in heaven,
may your name be held holy,
your kingdom come, your will be done,
on earth as in heaven.
Give us today our daily bread.
And forgive us our debts,
as we have forgiven those who are in debt to us.
And do not put us to the test,
but save us from the Evil One.

SILENCE

SONG OR CANTICLE
(sung, when possible; otherwise, spoken aloud with feeling)

The Spirit of God at Work
Isaiah 61:1-3, 11

REFRAIN
The LORD has anointed me;
and sent me to bring good news to the oppressed.

The spirit of the LORD GOD is upon me,
because the LORD has anointed me;

he has sent me to bring good news to the
  oppressed, to bind up the brokenhearted,
to proclaim liberty to the captives, and release
  to the prisoners;
to proclaim the year of the LORD's favor, and
  the day of vengeance of our God;
to comfort all who mourn; to provide for
  those who mourn in Zion—
to give them a garland instead of ashes, the oil
  of gladness instead of mourning,
  the mantle of praise instead of a faint spirit.
They will be called oaks of righteousness,
  the planting of the LORD, to display his glory.
For as the earth brings forth its shoots, and as
  a garden causes what is sown in it to spring up,
so the LORD God will cause righteousness and
  praise to spring up before all the nations.

The LORD has anointed me;
and sent me to bring good news to the oppressed.

PSALM
(chanted, when possible; otherwise, spoken aloud)

Psalm 132:1-5, 8-10

LORD, remember David,
  and all the hardships he endured;
How he swore an oath to the LORD
  and vowed a vow to the Mighty One of Jacob:

"I will not come under the roof of my house,
   nor climb up into my bed;
I will not allow my eyes to sleep,
   nor let my eyelids slumber;
Until I find a place for the LORD,
   a dwelling for the Mighty One of Jacob."
Arise, O LORD, into your resting-place,
   you and the ark of your strength.
Let your priests be clothed with righteousness;
   let your faithful people sing with joy.
For your servant David's sake,
   do you turn away the face of your Anointed.

GOSPEL READING

Matthew 10:27-32

HEAR THE WORD OF THE LORD: Jesus said to the twelve disciples: "What I say to you in the dark, tell in the daylight; what you hear in whispers, proclaim from the housetops. Do not be afraid of those who kill the body but cannot kill the soul; fear him rather who can destroy both body and soul in hell. Can you not buy two sparrows for a penny? And yet not one falls to the ground without your Father knowing. Why, every hair on your head has been counted. So there is not need to be afraid; you are worth more than many sparrows. So if anyone declares himself for me in the presence of human beings, I will declare myself for him in the presence of my Father in heaven."

SILENCE

PRAYERS OF THE SAINTS

O wondrous condescension of the divine mercy for us! How boundless the depths of God's love, which sacrificed a Son to ransom a slave! Yet God does not withhold the gifts of his compassion, but still protects with continual care the vineyard his right hand has planted. Even at the eleventh hour, God has sent workers to cultivate it, root out briars and thorns with hoe and plowshare. These men and women have cut back the overgrown branches and pulled up the brambles and shallow-rooted offshoots so that the vines might produce sweet fruit. Such fruit, when purified in the winepress of endurance, can be stored in the cellar of eternity. Amen.

—*Pope Gregory IX,*
friend and advisor to St. Francis

COLLECT

Grant your servants, O God, to be set on fire
with your Spirit, strengthened by your power,
illuminated by your splendor, filled with your grace,
and to go forward by your aid.
Give us, O Lord, a right faith, perfect love,
  true humility.
Grant, O Lord, that there may be in us simple
  affection,
brave patience, persevering obedience, perpetual
  peace, a pure mind,
a right and clean heart, a good will,
  a holy conscience, spiritual compunction,
spiritual strength, a life unspotted and upright;
and after having finished our course,
  may we be happily enabled
to enter into your kingdom. Amen.
  —*Gallican Sacramentary*

MORNING PRAYER

Friday

*Theme/Intent:
Passion More Important than Learning)*

PREPARATION

Christ, have mercy upon us.
Christ, save us from our sins.
Your love has no bounds,
and neither shall ours, with your help.
You are the lamp for our path and
the light within us.

GOSPEL SENTENCE

Luke 12:49

OUR LORD JESUS CHRIST, SAYS: I have come to bring fire to the earth, and how I wish it were blazing already!

CONFESSION

Have Mercy on Me, O God
(from Psalm 51)

Have mercy on me, O God, according to your
  loving-kindness;
  in your great compassion blot out my offenses.
Wash me through and through from my
  wickedness
  and cleanse me from my sin.
For I know my transgressions,
  and my sin is ever before me.
Create in me a clean heart, O God,
  and renew a right spirit within me.
Cast me not away from your presence
  and take not your holy Spirit from me.
Give me the joy of your saving help again
  and sustain me with your bountiful Spirit.
Deliver me from death, O God,
  and my tongue shall sing of your righteousness,
  O God of my salvation.

SILENCE

SONG OR CANTICLE
(sung, when possible; otherwise, spoken aloud with feeling)

Isaiah's Song for Righteousness
Isaiah 2:2-5

REFRAIN
Come, let us walk in the light of the LORD!

In days to come the mountain of the LORD's house
    shall be established as the highest of the
    mountains, and shall be raised above the hills;
all the nations shall stream to it. Many peoples
    shall come and say,
"Come, let us go up to the mountain of the
    LORD, to the house of the God of Jacob;
that he may teach us his ways and that we
    may walk in his paths."
For out of Zion shall go forth instruction, and
    the word of the LORD from Jerusalem.
He shall judge between the nations,
    and shall arbitrate for many peoples;
they shall beat their swords into plowshares,
    and their spears into pruning hooks;
nation shall not lift up sword against nation,
    neither shall they learn war any more.
O house of Jacob, come,
    let us walk in the light of the LORD!

Come, let us walk in the light of the LORD!

(chanted, when possible; otherwise, spoken aloud)

Psalm 119:12-19

Blessed are you, O LORD;
  instruct me in your statutes.
With my lips will I recite
  all the judgments of your mouth.
I have taken greater delight in the way of your
  decrees than in all manner of riches.
I will meditate on your commandments,
  and give attention to your ways.
My delight is in your statutes;
  I will not forget your word.
Deal bountifully with your servant,
  that I may live and keep your word.
Open my eyes, that I may see
  the wonders of your law.
I am a stranger here on earth;
  do not hide your commandments from me.

GOSPEL READING

Luke 7:31-35

HEAR THE WORD OF THE LORD: Jesus said: "What comparison, then, can I find for the people of this generation? What are they like? They are like children shouting to one another while they sit in the market place: 'We played the pipes for you, and you wouldn't dance; we sang dirges, and you wouldn't cry.' For John the Baptist has come, not eating bread, not drinking wine, and you say, 'He is possessed.' The Son of man has come, eating and drinking, and you say, 'Look, a glutton and a drunkard, a friend of tax collectors and sinners.' Yet wisdom is justified by all her children."

SILENCE

PRAYERS OF THE SAINTS

Give me, O Lord, pure lips, a clean and innocent heart, humility, courage, patience. Give me the Spirit of wisdom and understanding, the Spirit of counsel and strength, the Spirit of knowledge and godliness, and of the fear of God. Help me to always seek your face with all of my heart, all of my soul, and all of my mind. Grant me to have a contrite and humble heart in your presence. Most high, eternal, and ineffable Wisdom, drive away from me the darkness of blindness and ignorance. Most high and eternal Strength, deliver me. Most high and eternal Light, illuminate me. Most high and infinite Mercy, have mercy on me. Amen.
　　—*Gallican Sacramentary*

COLLECT

Good Shepherd
and Guardian of our souls,
we adore you.
We adore you in
Spirit and in truth.
Let us not lose heart,
except to make more room for
you in our hearts. Amen.

EVENING PRAYER
Friday

Theme/Intent:
Passion More Important than Learning)

PREPARATION

Blessed Holy One,
Lover of my youth,
draw me after you, and I will come.
I long for your affection, your embrace
and your kiss.
You are Most Beautiful, my Beloved;
I will sing your praises.

GOSPEL SENTENCE

Luke 10:25-28

A READING FROM THE GOSPEL ACCORDING TO
LUKE: And now a lawyer stood up and, to test
Jesus, asked, "Master, what must I do to inherit
eternal life?" He said to him, "What is written in

the Law? What is your reading of it?" He replied, "You must love the Lord your God with all your heart, with all your soul, with all your strength, and with all your mind, and your neighbor as yourself." Jesus said to him, "You have answered right, do this and life is yours."

Trisagion, an ancient Lenten prayer
(said three times)

Holy God,
Holy and Mighty,
Holy Immortal One,
Have mercy upon us.

SILENCE

Jeremiah's Song of Hope
Jeremiah 14:9b, 20-21, 22b

REFRAIN
You are in the midst of us;
we set our hope on you.

You, O LORD, are in the midst of us,
  and we are called by your name;
  do not forsake us!
We acknowledge our wickedness,
O LORD, the iniquity of our ancestors, for
  we have sinned against you.
Do not spurn us, for your name's sake;
  do not dishonor your glorious throne;
remember and do not break your
  covenant with us.
We set our hope on you

  You are in the midst of us;
  we set our hope on you.

PSALM
(chanted, when possible; otherwise, spoken aloud)

Psalm 31:1-5

In you, O LORD, have I taken refuge;
let me never be put to shame:
  deliver me in your righteousness.

Incline your ear to me;
    make haste to deliver me.
Be my strong rock, a castle to keep me safe,
for you are my crag and my stronghold;
    for the sake of your Name,
    lead me and guide me.
Take me out of the net that they have secretly
    set for me,
    for you are my tower of strength.
Into your hands I commend my spirit,
    for you have redeemed me,
    O LORD, O God of truth.

GOSPEL READING

Luke 11:9-13

HEAR THE WORD OF THE LORD: "So I say to you: 'Ask, and it will be given to you; search, and you will find; knock, and the door will be opened to you. For everyone who asks receives; everyone who searches finds; everyone who knocks will have the door opened. What father among you, if his son asked for a fish, would hand him a snake? Or if he asked for an egg, hand him a scorpion? If you then, evil as you are, know how to give your children what is good, how much more will the heavenly Father give the Holy Spirit to those who ask him!'"

PRAYERS OF THE SAINTS

'Lord hear my prayer' (Ps. 60:2) that my soul may not collapse (Ps. 83:3) under your discipline (Ps. 54:2), and may not suffer exhaustion in confessing to you your mercies, by which you have delivered me from all my evil ways. Bring to me a sweetness surpassing all the seductive delights which I pursued. Enable me to love you with all my strength that I may clasp your hand with all my heart.

   —*St. Augustine of Hippo*

COLLECT

Guide us in your way, O Christ,
and mercifully show the fountain of wisdom
to our thirsting minds;
that we may be free from sorrowful heaviness,
and may drink in the sweetness of life eternal.
Amen.

MORNING PRAYER
Saturday
(Theme/Intent: Joyful Simplicity)

PREPARATION

O Holy Christ, our shepherd,
we bleet before you.
O Holy Ghost, our inspiration,
we dance before you.
O Holy One,
even our foolishness brings you praise.

GOSPEL SENTENCE

Matthew 6:27-29

OUR LORD JESUS CHRIST, SAYS: Can any of you,
however much you worry, add one single cubit to
your span of life? And why worry about clothing?
Think of the flowers growing in the fields; they
never have to work or spin; yet I assure you that
not even Solomon in all his royal robes was
clothed like one of these.

CONFESSION

Have Mercy on Me, O God
(from Psalm 51)

Have mercy on me, O God,
   according to your loving-kindness;
   in your great compassion blot out my offenses.
Wash me through and through from my
   wickedness and cleanse me from my sin.
For I know my transgressions,
   and my sin is ever before me.
Create in me a clean heart, O God,
   and renew a right spirit within me.
Cast me not away from your presence
   and take not your holy Spirit from me.
Give me the joy of your saving help again
   and sustain me with your bountiful Spirit.
Deliver me from death, O God,
   and my tongue shall sing of your
   righteousness,
   O God of my salvation.

SILENCE

A Song for the Messiah
Isaiah 9:2-7

REFRAIN
Those who lived in a land of deep darkness—
on them light has shined.

The people who walked in darkness have seen
a great light;
those who lived in a land of deep darkness—
on them light has shined.
You have multiplied the nation,
you have increased its joy;
they rejoice before you as with joy at the harvest,
as people exult when dividing plunder.
For the yoke of their burden,
and the bar across their shoulders,
the rod of their oppressor, you have broken as
on the day of Midian.
For all the boots of the tramping warriors and
all the garments rolled in blood
shall be burned as fuel for the fire.
For a child has been born for us,
a son given to us;
authority rests upon his shoulders;
and he is named
Wonderful Counselor, Mighty God,
Everlasting Father, Prince of Peace.
His authority shall grow continually,
and there shall be endless peace

for the throne of David and his kingdom.
   He will establish and uphold it
with justice and with righteousness from this
   time onward and forevermore.
The zeal of the LORD of hosts will do this.

   Those who lived in a land of deep darkness—
      on them light has shined.

PSALM
(chanted, when possible; otherwise, spoken aloud)

Psalm 105:1-4

Give thanks to the LORD and call upon his Name;
   make known his deeds among the peoples.
Sing to him, sing praises to him,
   and speak of all his marvelous works.
Glory in his holy Name;
   let the hearts of those who seek the LORD
   rejoice.
Search for the LORD and his strength;
   continually seek his face.

GOSPEL READING

Mark 6:35-43

HEAR THE WORD OF THE LORD: By now it was
getting very late, and his disciples came up to him

and said, "This is a lonely place and it is getting very late, so send them away, and they can go to the farms and villages round about, to buy themselves something to eat." He replied, "Give them something to eat yourselves." They answered, "Are we to go and spend two hundred denarii on bread for them to eat?" He asked, "How many loaves have you? Go and see." And when they had found out they said, "Five, and two fish." Then he ordered them to get all the people to sit down in groups on the green grass, and they sat down on the ground in squares of hundreds and fifties. Then he took the five loaves and the two fish, raised his eyes to heaven and said the blessing; then he broke the loaves and began handing them to his disciples to distribute among the people. He also shared out the two fish among them all. They all ate as much as they wanted. They collected twelve basketfuls of scraps of bread and pieces of fish.

SILENCE

PRAYERS OF THE SAINTS

Let there be no doubt about your possession of the kingdom of heaven. Let there be no hesitation among you! For you already possess a promise of a future inheritance and have received the pledge of the Spirit. Signed with the seal of Christ's glory, you respond in everything, by his grace, like those of that first school which he established upon coming into the world. For what they did in his presence, you have thoroughly begun to do in his absence.

—*attributed to Caesar of Speyer*

COLLECT

Heavenly Father, by your
blessed Holy Spirit, lead us.
Ghost of God, show us the way.
Guide us to your orchards of luscious fruit:
love, joy, peace, patience, gentleness, goodness,
faith, meekness, temperance,
and these will be our law. Amen.

EVENING PRAYER

Saturday

(Theme/Intent: Joyful Simplicity)

PREPARATION

Let us praise the divine mysteries of our faith.
Our joy rests in God and all of God's glory.
Beneath what troubles our hearts, our lives,
we are simple, we are God's.

GOSPEL SENTENCE

Matthew 7:21

OUR LORD, JESUS CHRIST, SAYS: It is not anyone
who says to me, "Lord, Lord," who will enter the
kingdom of Heaven, but the person who does the
will of my Father in heaven.

CONFESSION

The *Our Father*
(Matthew 6:9-13)

Our Father in heaven,
may your name be held holy,
your kingdom come, your will be done,
on earth as in heaven.
Give us today our daily bread.
And forgive us our debts,
as we have forgiven those who are in debt to us.
And do not put us to the test,
but save us from the Evil One.

SILENCE

SONG OR CANTICLE
(sung, when possible; otherwise, spoken aloud with feeling)

The Lord Will Shine on You
Isaiah 60:1-2, 18-20

REFRAIN
Your light has come,
and the glory of the LORD has risen upon you.

Arise, shine; for your light has come,
and the glory of the LORD has risen upon you.
For darkness shall cover the earth,

and thick darkness the peoples;
but the LORD will arise upon you,
   and his glory will appear over you.
Violence shall no more be heard in your land,
   devastation or destruction within your borders;
you shall call your walls Salvation,
   and your gates Praise.
The sun shall no longer be your light by day,
   nor for brightness shall the moon give light
   to you by night;
but the LORD will be your everlasting light, and
   your God will be your glory.
Your sun shall no more go down, or your
   moon withdraw itself;
for the LORD will be your everlasting light,
   and your days of mourning shall be ended.

Your light has come,
and the glory of the LORD has risen upon you.

PSALM
(chanted, when possible; otherwise, spoken aloud)

Psalm 134

Behold now, bless the LORD,
   all you servants of the LORD,
   you that stand by night in the house of
   the LORD.

Lift up your hands in the holy place
and bless the LORD;
the LORD who made heaven and earth
bless you out of Zion.

GOSPEL READING

Luke 10:38-42

HEAR THE WORD OF THE LORD: In the course of their journey Jesus came to a village, and a woman named Martha welcomed him into her house. She had a sister called Mary, who sat down at the Lord's feet and listened to him speaking. Now Martha, who was distracted with all the serving, came to him and said, "Lord, do you not care that my sister is leaving me to do the serving all by myself? Please tell her to help me." But the Lord answered, "Martha, Martha," he said, "you worry and fret about so many things, and yet few are needed, indeed only one. It is Mary who has chosen the better part, and it is not to be taken from her."

SILENCE

Do not be daunted immediately by fear and run away from the road that leads to salvation. It is bound to be narrow at the outset. But as we progress in this way of life and in faith, we shall run on the path of God's commandments, our hearts overflowing with the inexpressible delight of love. Amen.

—*St. Benedict of Nursia*, Prologue to the *Rule*

COLLECT

O Lord God, Light of the faithful,
Strength of those who labor,
the Resting Place for those who have died:
Grant us a tranquil night free from worry,
and after quiet sleep may we, by your bounty,
at the return of light,
be given new activity by the Holy Spirit,
once again to give thanks to you.
Amen.

OCCASIONAL PRAYERS
of Francis

THE LORD'S PRAYER
(Francis's expanded version)

THE FOLLOWING EXPANDED VERSION of one of our most familiar prayers was written by St. Francis. *The Mirror of Perfection*, a compilation of stories about Francis, many of them written by his own beloved Brother Leo, relates in the eighty-second chapter that Francis taught this long, beautiful version of the Lord's Prayer to his brothers.

OUR FATHER,
Most Holy, our Creator and Redeemer, our Savior and our Comforter.

WHO ART IN HEAVEN:
Together with the angels and the saints, giving them light so that they may have knowledge of you, because you, Lord, are Light; inflaming them so that they may love, because you, Lord, are Love; living continually in them and filling them so that they may be happy, because you, Lord, are the supreme good, the eternal good, and it is from you that all good comes, and without you there is no good.

HALLOWED BE THY NAME.
May our knowledge of you become ever clearer, so that we may realize the width and breadth of your blessings, the steadfastness of your promises, the sublimity of your majesty and the depth of your judgments.

THY KINGDOM COME,
So that you may reign in us by your grace and bring us to your Kingdom, where we will see you clearly, love you perfectly, be blessed in your presence, and enjoy you forever.

THY WILL BE DONE IN EARTH
AS IT IS IN HEAVEN:

So that we may love you with our whole heart by always thinking of you; directing our whole intention with our whole mind towards you and seeking your glory in everything; spending all our powers and affections of soul and body with all our strength in the service of your love alone. May we also love our neighbors as ourselves, encouraging them to love you as best we can, rejoicing at the good fortune of others, just as if it were our own, and sympathizing with their misfortunes, giving offense to no one.

GIVE US THIS DAY OUR DAILY BREAD,
Your own beloved Son, our Lord Jesus Christ, so to remind us of the love he showed for us and to help us understand and appreciate it and everything that he did or said or suffered.

AND FORGIVE US OUR TRESPASSES,
In your infinite mercy, and by the power of
the Passion of your Son, our Lord Jesus
Christ, together with the merits and the
intercession of the Blessed Virgin Mary
and all your saints.

AS WE FORGIVE
THOSE WHO TRESPASS AGAINST US,
And if we do not forgive perfectly, Lord,
make us do so, so that we may indeed love
our enemies out of our love for you, and
pray fervently to you for them, never
returning evil for evil, anxious only to serve
everybody in you.

AND LEAD US NOT INTO TEMPTATION.
Neither hidden or obvious, sudden or
unforeseen.

BUT DELIVER US FROM EVIL—
Present, past, or to come.
Amen.

SONGS OF JOY
IN THE MORNING
AND EVENING

FRANCIS REFINED "The Canticle of Brother Sun"
over the course of several years. He and his
companions would sing it from time to time to
cheer themselves up, to bless the creatures of the
earth, or simply to praise God. Its themes show

Francis to be carefully tuned to the world around him, in loving relationship to the many aspects of God. While this complete prayer is reproduced in its entirety below (see pp. 128-130), here are two songs derived from Francis's *Canticle* for morning and evening.

A Song in the Morning

Glory to God, source of all being;
to you belong praise, glory, honor,
and all blessing!
Blessed be our Lord and all of the creatures.
Bless Brother Sun,
who brings us the day, brings us the light.
Illumine our day, make bright our way!
Brother Sun never fails,
shining with great splendor.
Glory to God, source of all being. Amen.

A Song in the Evening

Glory to God, source of all things;
to you belong praise, glory, honor,
and all blessing!
Praised be God for Sister Death of the Body;
we cannot escape her.
Blessed are they who walk by God's holy will,
for the second death
has no power to do them harm.
Bless the Lord for creating Sister Death.
Glory to God, source of all things. Amen.

PRAYER FOR
DOING GOD'S WILL

THE AUTHORS OF *The Legend of the Three Companions,* one of the earliest biographical documents written about St. Francis, first recorded this brief prayer spoken by the young saint as he kneeled in the old ruined church of San Damiano before the crucifix that would later become famous for "speaking" to him, telling him what to do. It is the earliest prayer of St. Francis that we have handed down to us.

Most High
and glorious God,
enlighten the darkness of my heart
and give me
truer faith,
more certain hope,
and perfect charity,
sense and knowledge
of you,
so that I may carry out
your holy and true command
for my life.

PRAYER FOR DETACHMENT

THE *Poverello* beautifully combined in his spirituality a love for the Creation and all of its manifestations with a traditional mystic's love for detachment from everything but God. In John of the Cross and John Cassian we see only the latter; in Dante we see only the former; in Francis's life these two seemingly incompatible facets of spiritual understanding seem as easy parts of a whole. Where "The Canticle of Brother Sun" is his song for God's many-splendored Creation, the following prayer shows Francis turning his face straight toward heaven, although with metaphors very much from earth.

(The early fourteenth-century leader of the "Spiritual" Franciscans, Ubertino of Casale, attests to this prayer's authenticity, but some contemporary scholars disagree.)

O Lord Jesus Christ,
I pray you that the fiery and honey-sweet
power of your love may detach my soul
from everything under heaven,
so that I may die for love of your love,
who out of love for your people
did die on the tree of the cross. Amen.

PRAYER TO THE VIRGIN MARY, *THEOTOKOS* (Mother of God)

FRANCIS'S DEVOTION TO MARY was deeply felt throughout his adult life. The images used here— handmaid, mother, spouse—each correspond in Mary's ministry to one of the persons of the Trinity.

Holy Virgin Mary,
There is none like you
among all women on earth.
You are the daughter and
handmaid of the Most High King and
Father of Heaven.
You are the mother of our most holy Lord
Jesus Christ.
You are the spouse of the Holy Spirit.
Pray for us, with Saint Michael the Archangel
and all the powers of heaven
and all the saints,
to your most holy and beloved Son,
Our Lord and Master.
Glory to the Father and to the Son,
and to the Holy Spirit.
Amen.

PRAYER FOR EXUBERANT FAITH

THE PENULTIMATE CHAPTER in the first version of
Francis's Rule is a long prayer of one hundred and
sixty-five lines. The first half chronicles the basic
tenets of the Apostle's Creed and asks for the
perseverance of all Christians in faith. The second
half is by far the more lovely and moving. It
articulates the exuberant faith that Francis desired
for himself and his brothers; it builds a beautiful
momentum from beginning to end. This version
is an adaptation from the original.

I.

With our whole heart, soul, mind, strength,
and fortitude;
with our whole understanding, powers, effort,
affection, and feeling;
with every desire and wish,
let us love the Lord our God
who gives each of us our body, our soul, our life;
who creates, redeems, and saves us by mercy alone;
who does all good for us, the miserable, wretched,
rotten, and ungrateful.

II.

Let us desire nothing else, want nothing else,
delight in nothing else,
except our Creator, Redeemer, and Savior
who alone is good; who alone is holy.
Let nothing hinder, separate, or come between us.
Wherever we are, in every place, hour,
and time of day,
let us continually, truly, and humbly hold in
our heart and love
the Most High, Trinity and Unity, Father, Son, and
Holy Spirit.

III.

Creator of all, Savior of all,
we believe in, hope in, and love you.
Unchangeable, invisible,
unspeakable, unfathomable,
you alone are most gentle, most lovable,
most delightful, and totally desirable
above all others! Amen.

A BENEDICTION OF ST. FRANCIS

TAKEN FROM THE SAME CHAPTER OF FRANCIS'S RULE as are the prayers immediately above, we also have this beautiful benediction penned by the saint.

Now, wherever we are,
and in every place,
and at every hour,
throughout each time of each day,
may all of us honestly and humbly believe,
holding in our hearts
to love, honor,
adore, serve,
praise, bless,
glorify, exalt,
magnify, and give thanks
to the Most High and Eternal God,
Trinity and Unity.
Amen.

PRAYER FOR
A RICH SPIRITUAL LIFE

THE FOLLOWING PRAYER, written by Francis late in life, is probably the best summary we have of his spiritual concerns. In praying this prayer, we can draw on the spirit of Francis of Assisi in our attempt to live a meaningful life before God.

In the manuscript tradition of his writings, "Almighty, eternal, just, and merciful God" is often appended to the letter that Francis wrote to the Franciscan brothers, its leaders, and future leaders, laying out his priorities for the Order beyond his death. It is most likely for that reason— and simply because of the beauty and completeness of it—that these words encompass all of Francis's spiritual priorities.

Almighty, eternal, just, and merciful God,
grant to us miserable ones the grace to do for you
what we know you want us to do.
Give us always to desire what pleases you.
Inwardly cleansed, interiorly illumined
and enflamed with the fire of the Holy Spirit,
may we be able to follow in the footprints
of your beloved Son, our Lord Jesus Christ,
and attain to you, Most High, by your grace alone,
who in perfect Trinity and simple Unity
lives and reigns and is glorified as God almighty,
forever and ever. Amen.

"THE CANTICLE OF BROTHER SUN"
(FRANCIS'S SONG OF JOY)

"THE CANTICLE OF BROTHER SUN" is Francis's most popular prayer, with the exception of "Lord, Make Me an Instrument of Thy Peace," which was not actually composed by him. The Canticle is a song to be sung; the brothers sang it for Francis at many crisis times in his life and the early life of the Franciscan movement. It sustained them and is remarkable for its affirmation of the elements of God's Creation.

Francis wrote this popular prayer song after a period of self-doubt, ill health, and despondency. In *The Road to Assisi: The Essential Biography of St. Francis,* Paul Sabatier explains what happened to the saint after he wrote "The Canticle of Brother Sun":

> Joy had returned to Francis, joy as deep as ever. For a whole week he put aside his breviary and passed his days in repeating "The Canticle of the Sun."
>
> During a night of sleeplessness he heard a voice saying to him, "If you had faith as a grain of mustard seed, you would say to this mountain, 'Be removed from here,' and it would move away." Was not the mountain his sufferings, the temptation to murmur and despair? "Be it, Lord, according to your word," Francis replied with all his heart, and immediately he felt that he was delivered.
>
> Francis might have perceived that the mountain had not greatly changed its place, but for several days he turned his eyes away from it and had been able to forget its existence.
>
> For a moment he thought of summoning to his side Brother Pacifico, the king of verse, to retouch his canticle. His idea was

to attach to him a certain number of friars who would go with him from village to village, preaching. After the sermon they would sing the hymn of the sun, and they were to close by saying to the gathered crowd, "We are God's jugglers. We desire to be paid for our sermon and our song. Our payment will be that you persevere in penitence."

"Is it not in fact true," Francis would add, "that the servants of God are really like jugglers, intended to revive the hearts of men and lead them into spiritual joy?"

The Francis of the old raptures was back —the layman, the poet, the artist.

"The Canticle of Brother Sun" represented many great things in Francis's life: Francis saw it as a gift from God, a recovery from his deeply felt self-doubts, and a revelation of what role he and his brothers were to play in the lives of the people they encountered. The joy of this simple song is unmatched. The earthiness—and the sanctifying of the earthy everyday-ness of life that comes by repeating it—was essential for Francis. Its influence in the early days of the Franciscan movement was great, as was its influence in the earliest moments of vernacular literature in Italy. This was Francis of Assisi's favorite of his prayers.

O most high, almighty, good Lord God, to you belong praise, glory, honor, and all blessing!

Praised be my Lord God with all your creatures,
and especially our Brother Sun,
who brings us the day and who brings us the light.
Fair is he and shines with a very great splendor:
O Lord, he signifies you to us!
Praised be my Lord for our Brother Wind,
and for air and cloud, calms and all weather
through which you uphold life in all creatures.
Praised be my Lord for our Sister Water,
who is very useful to us and humble
and precious and clean.
Praised be my Lord for our Brother Fire,
through whom you give us light in the darkness;
and he is bright and pleasant and very mighty and
strong.
Praised be my Lord for our Mother Earth,
who does sustain us and keep us,
and brings forth many fruits and flowers
of many colors, and grass.
Praised be my Lord for all those who pardon one
another for your sake,
and who endure weakness and tribulation;
blessed are they who peaceably endure, for you,
O most High,
shall give them a crown.
Praised be my Lord
for our Sister Death of the Body,
from whom no one can escape.
Woe to those who die in mortal sin.
Blessed are they
who are found walking by your most holy will,
for the second death

shall have no power to do them harm.
Praise and bless the Lord, and give thanks to him
and serve him with great humility.

MORE PRAYERS

ST. FRANCIS VERY OFTEN PRAYED BY HEART, which means that the words of prayers like those that follow reverberated inside of him. He memorized them, or he simply remembered them as a result of repetition, so that their words could be easily on his lips, and so that in mystical ways, they would pray themselves for him, inside of him, like our heart, which also beats involuntarily.

We can do the same. Here are some basic prayers for learning by heart. Each dates from the early centuries of the Christian Church and is today found in various forms throughout the world.

COLLECT FOR PURITY

Almighty God, to you all hearts are open,
all desires known,
and from you no secrets are hid:
Cleanse the thoughts of our hearts
by the inspiration of your Holy Spirit,   •
that we may perfectly love you, and worthily magnify your holy Name;
through Jesus Christ our Lord. Amen.

THE DOXOLOGY

Glory be to the Father, and to the Son,
and to the Holy Spirit.
As it was in the beginning,
is now and ever shall be,
world without end. Amen.

A PRAYER TO OUR LADY

O Mother of God,
we take refuge
in your loving care.
Let not our plea to you pass unheeded
in the trials that confront us,
but deliver us from danger.
For you alone are truly pure;
you alone are truly blessed.

THE JESUS PRAYER

Lord Jesus Christ,
Son of God,
have mercy on me, a sinner.

LORD, MAKE ME AN
INSTRUMENT OF YOUR PEACE

THIS PRAYER, surely the most recognized prayer

attributed to St. Francis, was not actually written by him or dictated by him to his brothers. Its author is in fact anonymous and the prayer is only about a century old. However, its lasting influence is due to how closely it reflects the true spirit of the *Poverello*.

Lord, make me an instrument of your peace.
Where there is hatred let me sow peace;
where there is injury let me sow forgiveness;
where there is doubt let me sow faith;
where there is despair let me give hope;
where there is darkness let me give light;
where there is sadness let me give joy.
O Lord,
grant that I may not try to be comforted
but to comfort,
not try to be understood but to understand,
not try to be loved but to love.
Because it is in giving that we receive,
it is in forgiving that we are forgiven,
and it is in dying that we are born
to eternal life.

IMPORTANT SAINTS' DAYS—
ST. FRANCIS AND ST. CLARE

THROUGHOUT THE YEAR, the Church calendar includes various kinds of feast days. Some feast days are for the purpose of remembering the lives of saints; they are a time to celebrate the life of a saint on the day that marks his or her death.

AUGUST 11
Traditional Prayer for the Feast Day of St. Clare

O God, whose blessed Son became poor that we through his poverty might be rich: Deliver us, we pray, from an inordinate love of this world, that, inspired by the devotion of your servant Clare, we may serve you with singleness of heart, and attain to the riches of the age to come; through Jesus Christ our Lord, who lives and reigns with you, in the unity of the Holy Spirit, one God, now and ever. Amen.

OCTOBER 4
*TraditionalPrayer for Animals
for the Feast Day of St. Francis*

God our heavenly Father, You created the world to serve humanity's needs and to lead them to you. By our own fault we have lost the beautiful relationship we once had with all your Creation. Help us to see that by restoring our relationship with you we will also restore it with all your Creation. Give us the grace to see all animals as gifts from you and to treat them with respect for they are your creation. We pray for all animals who are suffering as a result of our neglect. May the order you originally established be once again restored to the whole world through the intercession of the Glorious Virgin Mary, the prayers of St. Francis and the merits of your Son, Our Lord Jesus Christ, who lives and reigns with you, now and forever. Amen.

APPENDICES

THE USE OF DEVOTIONAL BOOKS
in Francis's Day

THE SMALL DEVOTIONAL BOOK OF TODAY had its beginnings in Europe in the centuries before St. Francis. As early as the eighth and ninth centuries, many examples were common, including Psalters (collections of the 150 Psalms from the Bible) with additional prayers; illuminated, or illustrated, editions of the Gospels with additional creeds and litanies of saints; breviaries for reciting the Divine Office; and emerging in Francis's century was the *primer*, or Book of Hours, which focused primarily on the spirituality of the Blessed Virgin. All of these devotional tools reflected the efforts of laypeople desiring to pray each day in ways similar to monks and nuns.

Francis wanted the spirituality of the cloister to be available to people everywhere. In fact, at the end of most of his writings, he encouraged his friars and others to make copies, adding: "Let those who keep this writing with them, and those who make copies of it to distribute and share with others, know that they will be greatly blessed by God." He wanted to publish the good news that he was preaching and teaching.

We know that Francis used books from time to time but they must have been very spare indeed. It is impossible to imagine books with ornamentation—gold gilded edges, elegant illuminations—allowed by the *Poverello* in the chapel of Portiuncula, in the convent of San Damiano, with the Brothers on the cliffs of La Verna, in the simple abodes of Rivo-Torto, or in the Carceri, those damp caves that he loved so much. This was a man who believed that the simple handling of coins was a sin for a friar married to Poverty. The personal owning of books represented to Francis both extravagance and arrogance.

These early devotional books were actually handbound manuscripts, often illuminated with beautiful colors and designs. Such books were usually owned or commissioned by wealthy patrons. For example, copies of the Gospels were fairly common in the Middle Ages and highly valued by those lucky enough to possess one. Cuthbert, the seventh-century bishop of Lindisfarne, was buried with his Gospel of John; the mystical—and valuable—text was found enclosed in his coffin.

But we also know that Francis used prayer books. Books were sometimes available in the community of friars for spiritual purposes. If Francis ever used a prayer book for private devotions, it was probably small and well-worn. It was surely borrowed or given to his young order secondhand, a copy previously owned by a wealthy monastery, discarded for the very plainness that attracted the newly converted son of Bernardone. It may have had beechwood boards, making it lighter and more portable than the oak wood boards commonly used for bound manuscripts in England in Francis's day.

The pages of devotional books were made of parchment—sheepskin, to be exact—because paper was not introduced widely in Italy until after the time of St. Francis. The boards—the rough equivalent of what we refer to as "hardcovers" today—were covered with animal skin, usually goat, calf, or sheep. We can imagine that the use of animal products added to Francis's displeasure with owning books. As he turned the pages, searching for the words of David to express his latest anguish or triumph, he would have felt the roughness of one side of each page, where the hair of the animal had originally been, and the comparative smoothness on the other where the flesh had been.

Finally, Thomas of Celano, friend and first biographer of St. Francis, wrote: "[Francis] always fulfilled his hours standing up straight and without a hood, without letting his eyes wander and with-out dropping syllables," revealing an important difference in public and private prayer from Francis's time to our own: Silent reading was uncommon until about the time of Francis. When Thomas writes that his master did not drop syllables, he knows this because, in Francis's day, even "private" prayer was public in the sense that it was spoken aloud. Imagine what it was like for Brother Leo and the other early Franciscans to listen in!

MEMORIZATION AND PRAYER IN THE
Middle Ages

Children, knowledge is a treasury and
your heart is its strongbox.
—Hugh of St. Victor,
in his treatise on the art of memory entitled
De Tribus Maximis Circumstantiis Gestorum

He sometimes read the Sacred Books,
and whatever he once put into his mind,
he wrote indelibly in his heart. His memory
took the place of books, because, if he
heard something once, it was not wasted,
as his heart would mull it over with constant
devotion. He said this was the fruitful way
to read and learn, rather than to wander
through a thousand treatises.
—Thomas of Celano,
in his second biography of St. Francis

THE PRIMARY FUNCTION OF LEARNING in medieval
Europe, before the growth of the first universities
in the twelfth and thirteenth centuries, was to
teach moral lessons. For this reason, people read,
or learned to read, primarily in order to memorize.
At a time when philosophy was rediscovered and
seen as useful only in its service to theology and to the

Church, reading was seen as useful only in its helpfulness to memorization and morality.

Memorization—the last remnant of which can still be found in our Sunday schools—was commonplace in ways that are hard to understand today. The Middle Ages inherited various intricate techniques for memorizing words on a page, dating from the days of Cicero in ancient Rome. These teachings were passed from teacher to student, and appeared in various written treatises on the subject by Cicero, Aristotle, Albertus Magnus— the early Dominican and teacher of Thomas Aquinas—and many others.

Large portions of the written word were committed to memory by creating pictures in the mind, background scenes on which the words, or images used to represent categories of words, were projected. These mental pictures were then rehearsed over and over until they could be remembered flawlessly. The most common image used to describe a good memory was a wax tablet or seal, a good image for the sort of indelible impression that was intended.

Writing, too, was a tool for memorization. Practicing letters, words, and sentences on a tablet were seen as perhaps the best of all possible methods for training the memory. As the psalmist who urges us to "Remember the word of the Lord," the child learning to write did so as moral practice, inscribing on the heart.

Finally, memory was intended to come to the service of good rhetoric (speechmaking) and persuasion. Some of Francis's contemporaries even saw divine origins to persuasive speech, for otherwise, how would Lucifer have convinced the other angels in heaven to follow him? Francis probably understood this connection, and his persuasiveness as a speaker was legendary. Just as he turned secular music to sacred ends, Francis also used the techniques of Cicero to preach the Good News.

INDEX OF SUBJECTS

INDEX OF SCRIPTURES

NOTE: Page numbers are in parentheses. Scripture books/chapters are in bold.

Philippians 1 (153 note)

Psalms 22 (45-46); **24** (85); **31** (102-103); **42** (62); **51** (38, 49, 60, 72, 83, 95, 106); **54** (104); **60** (104); **83** (104); **84** (74); **95** (51); **100** (56-57); **105** (108); **108** (40); **119** (9, 21, 97); **128** (22); **130** (22); **132** (90-91); **134** (113-114); **141** (79); **142** (22-23); **146** (67-68)

Samuel, First 2 (39)

*Tobit 13 (26, 61, 66-67)

* Those texts that are found in The Apocrypha, a collection of writings found in Roman Catholic Bibles but not in most Protestant Bibles, are noted here with an asterisk *. The disagreement regarding whether or not to include these texts in the official Scripture canon is ancient, dating back to debates in the early centuries of the Church. St. Francis knew these "apocryphal" scriptures, and quoted from them in his writings.

INDEX OF AUTHORS
AND SOURCES

NOTES

THE PRAYER LIFE OF FRANCIS OF ASSISI

p. 9. *"Seven times a day do I praise you."*
Translations used are as follows: Gospels, The New Jerusalem Bible; Psalms, *The Book of Common Prayer*, 1979; and Songs and Canticles from the Hebrew Bible, The New Revised Standard Version (with the exception of "The Song of the Three Young Men"—pg. 78-79—which is not found in the NRSV; the NJB is used for it, here).

p. 9. *Thomas of Celano...wrote: "When he was travelling..."*
Armstrong et al (eds.), *Francis of Assisi: Early Documents, Vol. 3;* (New York: New City Press, 2000), p. 311.

p. 10. *"Even when he was suffering from diseases..."*
Ibid., p. 311.

p. 11. *Brother Leo overheard Francis... "Who are You..."*
The Little Flowers of Saint Francis, trans. by Raphael Brown; p. 186.

p. 13. *"And at last he found Him," the text reads...*
Ibid., pp. 175-176.

p. 19. *Even prayer books, Francis believed...*
It is also worth noting that books, before paper, were extravagantly expensive. Francis did not want his Brothers to own their own books because of what books represented at that time. For example, more than two hundred years after the time of Francis, "It had been calculated that each copy of the Gutenberg Bible (641 leaves) printed on parchment required the skins of 300 sheep" (Hugh Kennedy, *Times Literary Supplement*, August 16, 2002). Francis's love for poverty and hate of pride were the two most important reasons for his strong opinion about the Brothers not possessing their own books.

p. 20. *Brother Giles...was able to say... "He who does..."*
The Little Flowers of Saint Francis, p. 278.

p. 21. *"You have rebuked the insolent..."*
This verse, and all of the Scripture quotations in this section, are quoted or referenced by St. Francis in the earliest and later versions of his Rule, and in his brief meditation of praises of God composed on La Verna, "The Canticle of Brother Sun." See Armstrong et al. (eds.), *Francis of Assisi, Vol. 1*; pp. 63–86, 99–106, and 108–109.

p. 22. *as when he instructed the Brothers to say....*
Francis's first Rule, chap. 3.

PRAYING ALONGSIDE ST. FRANCIS

p. 47. *Glorious God our Father / like old Simeon... / (Collect)*
This collect is based on Luke 2:29–32, what is commonly known in Latin as *Nunc Dimittis.*

p. 53. *Nicetas, fifth-century bishop of Remesiana...*
Remesiana is in modern Serbia. This prayer is the concluding portion of the ancient prayer, *Te Deum laudamus.*

p. 53. *Most High, glorious God / enlighten... / (Collect)*
This prayer resembles Francis's "Prayer before the Crucifix" originally prayed at San Damiano in Assisi early in the saint's religious life. See Armstrong et al. (eds.), *Francis of Assisi, Vol. 1*; p. 40.

p. 58. *Guigo the Carthusian (Prayer)*
Guigo II, "Ladder of Monks" in *The Ladder of Monks, A Letter on the Contemplative Life, and Twelve Meditations*, by Guigo II, trans. Edmund Colledge, O.S.A, and James Walsh, S.J. (Kalamazoo, MI: Cistercian Publications, 1979), p. 73. Guigo was a Carthusian monk and prior of the Carthusian mother house, the Grande Chartreuse. He wrote the *Ladder of Monks* and *Twelve Meditations*, but if St. Francis knew these great works, he probably knew them as the work of either Bernard of Clairvaux or St. Augustine, to whom they were often mistakenly attributed in the decades and early centuries after Guigo's death in 1188.

p. 58. *Blessed Lady Poverty / hidden... / (Collect)*
See "The Sacred Exchange Between St. Francis and Lady Poverty," in Armstrong et al. (eds.), *Francis of Assisi, Vol. 1*; pp. 529–554.

p. 64. *St. Bernard of Clairvaux (Prayer)*
This collect is based on Philippians 1:9-11.

p. 64. *Abba, Father / cleanse our hearts... / (Collect)*
On the Song of Songs I trans. Kilian Walsh O.C.S.O. (Kalamazoo, MI: Cisterian Publications, 1980), pp. 140–150.

p. 76. *Blessed Angela of Foligno (Prayer)*
From *Evangelical Doctrine*, chapter 15.

p. 76. *Bless the Lord / living and true! / (Collect)*
This collect is a slight adaptation of a prayer of Francis. See Armstrong et al. (eds.), *Francis of Assisi, Vol. 1*; p. 141.

p. 77. *Almighty and everlasting God... (Preparation)*
From the Gelasian Sacramentary.

p. 81. *Brother Jacopone of Todi (Prayer)*
From *The Lauds*, lxxxvi. See the original Italian and literal prose translation in *The Fool of God: Jacopone da Todi*, by George T. Peck (Birmington: The University of Alabama Press, 1980), p. 161.

p. 82. *Make us, O Lord, to flourish... (Preparation)*
From the Mozarabic Sacramentary.

p. 86. *St. Hildegard of Bingen (Prayer)*
Slightly adapted from *The Letters of Hildegard of Bingen, Vol. 1*, trans. Joseph L. Baird and Radd K. Ehrman (New York: Oxford University Press, 1994), p. 183.

p. 92. *Pope Gregory IX (Prayer)*
From his 1228 document proclaiming Francis of Assisi a saint.

p. 99. *Good Shepherd / and Guardian of our souls / (Collect)*
Adapted from Francis's first Rule, chap. xxii, 27–32, as well as John 4:23-24.

p. 104. *St. Augustine of Hippo (Prayer)*
Augustine, *Confessions*, trans. Henry Chadwick (New York:
Oxford University Press, 1991), pp. 17-18.

p. 104. *Guide us in your way, O Christ / (Collect)*
From the Mozarabic Sacramentary.

p. 110. *Caesar of Speyer (Prayer)*
From "The Sacred Exchange between St. Francis and Lady
Poverty". See Armstrong et al. (eds.), *Francis of Assisi, Vol. 1*;
p. 553.

p. 110. *Heavenly Father, by your / (Collect)*
This collect is based on Galatians 5:16.

p. 115. *St. Benedict of Nursia (Prayer)*
The Rule of St. Benedict (Collegeville, MN: The Liturgical
Press, 1981), prologue 48-49.

p. 115. *O Lord God, Light of the faithful / (Collect)*
From the Mozarabic Sacramentary.

OCCASIONAL PRAYERS OF FRANCIS

p. 124. *"O Lord Jesus Christ / I pray you that the fiery and
honey-sweet"*
See *St. Francis of Assisi: His Life and Writings as Recorded by
His Contemporaries*, trans. Leo Sherley-Price (New York:
Harper & Brothers, 1960), p. 166.

p. 126. *"Almighty, eternal, just, and merciful God"*
The Franciscan Prayerbook (www.franciscan-archive.org)
titles this prayer "Prayer for Final Perseverance." This version
is a combination of their public domain translation and the one
found in Armstrong et al. (eds.), *Francis of Assisi, Vol. 1*; pp.
120-121.

p. 128. *"Joy had returned to Francis, joy as deep as ever."*
Paul Sabatier, *The Road to Assisi: The Essential Biography of St.
Francis*, ed. Jon M. Sweeney (Orleans, MA: Paraclete Press,
2003), pp. 136–137.

MORE PRAYERS

p. 131. *Almighty God, to you all hearts are open... (Collect)*
This version from the *Book of Common Prayer*, from the first
edition (1549) in the Church of England to the most recent
in the Episcopal Church in the United States (1979), is used
throughout the Anglican Communion.

APPENDICES

p. 138. *Cuthbert, the seventh-century bishop of Lindisfarne...*
Peter Hunter Blair, *Roman Britain and Early England 55 B.C.
– A.D. 871* (New York: W.W. Norton, 1966), p. 212.

p. 141. *"He sometimes read the Sacred Books..."*
Armstrong et al. (eds.), *Francis of Assisi, Vol. 2*; p. 314.

p. 143. *how would Lucifer have convinced the other angels...*
Frances A. Yates, *The Art of Memory* (Chicago: Univ. of
Chicago Press, 1966), pp. 57-58.